a blues life

Music in American Life

A list of books in the series appears at the end of this book.

a blues

HENRY TOWNSEND

Life

As Told to BILL GREENSMITH

University of Illinois Press *Urbana & Chicago*

Library of Congress
Cataloging-in-Publication Data
Townsend, Henry.
A blues life / Henry Townsend as told to Bill
Greensmith.
    p. cm. — (Music in American life)
Includes discography (p.   ), bibliographical
references (p.   ), and index.
ISBN 0-252-02526-1 (acid-free paper)
1. Townsend, Henry. 2. Guitarists—Missouri—
Saint Louis Biography. 3. Blues musicians—
Missouri—Saint Louis Biography. I. Greensmith,
Bill, 1949–   II. Title. III. Series.
ML419.T68A3   1999
781.643'092—ddc21   99-6216
[B]   CIP

C 5 4 3 2 1

CONTENTS

Acknowledgments *ix*

Introduction *xi*

1 "Like a Bullet" *1*

2 "The Sweetest Guitar I've Ever Played" *20*

3 "Revenge Is Sweet" *31*

4 "Have Fun with It" *51*

5 "The Music Is a Mind Disturber" *65*

6 "A Very Good Hustle" *88*

7 "Making It Pretty Don't Help a Bit" *101*

Notes *113*

Discography *127*

Bibliography *139*

Index *141*

Illustrations follow page 50

ACKNOWLEDGMENTS *Bill Greensmith*

I am indebted to many people whose work I referred
to while working on this project. Paul Oliver, Charley
O'Brien, and Sam Charters were among the enlightened
who were responsible for groundbreaking research in the
late 1950s and early 1960s on St. Louis. In addition, Sam
Charters produced excellent albums on Henry Townsend
and Barrelhouse Buck. In the 1970s Mike Rowe unearthed
more gems, including the pianist Joe Dean, and along with
Charley O'Brien revealed information on the Sparks
Brothers, all of which was published in *Blues Unlimited.*

Much new and confidential material in the St. Louis
Police Department files was made available to me by an
anonymous source. This information helped shine a little
more light on artists who were, and in some cases still are,
biographical question marks. Where possible I have
incorporated this information into the notes.

My Bible throughout this whole project has been
Robert Dixon and John Godrich's *Blues and Gospel Records,
1902–43.* Without this invaluable reference tool life would
have been very different.

Thanks are also due to Paul Garon, Doug Seroff, and
Charley O'Brien for the loan of photographs from their
collections, to Sister Dionysia Brockland for the photographs from the Swekosky Collection, to Ann Morris at
UMSL for her enthusiasm and encouragement, and to
Doris Wesley and Stella Greensmith for typing the manu-
script.

INTRODUCTION *Bill Greensmith*

Since the early years of the century St. Louis and the neigh-
boring city of East St. Louis have boasted thriving blues communi-
ties. They have both enjoyed two distinct and diverse periods of pros-
perity, most notably the decade immediately before World War II and
the period between the years 1954 and 1966. Henry Townsend, who
first arrived in St. Louis in 1919 and began playing guitar in the mid-
1920s, was an integral part of the blues scene in St. Louis during its
formative years.

The St. Louis of Henry Townsend's youth was a vastly different
place from that of today. In the early part of the twentieth century
St. Louis was the fourth largest city in the United States and an important river town with a large industrial base. The economy of East
St. Louis was also flourishing, with a large percentage of its workforce
employed in the stockyards and steel foundries, whose chimneys dot-
ted the skyline. East St. Louis was also one of the largest railroad
junctions in the world and served as a major hub for many railroad
companies. It was the promise of jobs and the hope for opportuni-
ties that could never be realized under the oppressive Jim Crow system in the South that brought most black people to northern cities
such as Detroit, Chicago, and St. Louis. And along with them came
their music.

In his autobiography, W. C. Handy recalled being in St. Louis in
1893 and observing a couple of guitar players sing the tune "East St.
Louis," the form of which we now know to be a blues. In 1893 the style
was most certainly in its infancy, even if you choose to believe the
romantic visions of Handy. However, what we can be sure of is that
by the early 1920s the style was fully formed and St. Louis had an
abundance of blues artists.

At the time blues artists in St. Louis were establishing themselves,
Prohibition had taken a firm grip upon the nation. Although this in
itself did not stop people from drinking, it did reduce the opportuni-
ties for musicians who would otherwise make money by playing in
taverns and bars. The Prohibition laws effectively drove the music

underground, as house parties and private clubs became the order of the day. In East St. Louis, which was considered a more wide-open town because of its reputation of corruption and lawlessness, the Prohibition laws were often openly flaunted.

With few legitimate jobs, it is surprising that anyone managed to attract the attention of the record companies. Doubtless encouraged by their discovery in 1925 of the urbane and influential guitarist Lonnie Johnson, however, record companies began to focus further attention upon St. Louis artists. By 1930 many of the St. Louis artists of consequence had made their recording debuts: the pianists Roosevelt Sykes, Henry Brown, Sylvester Palmer, Wesley Wallace, Joe Dean, and Walter Davis; the vocalists Alice Moore, Mary Johnson, and Luella Miller; and the guitar players Clifford Gibson, Charley Jordan, Peetie Wheatstraw, and Henry Townsend. (Wheatstraw, like Henry Townsend, also played excellent piano.) Artists such as Roosevelt Sykes, Lonnie Johnson, Walter Davis, and Peetie Wheatstraw went on to enjoy extended and prolific recording careers, but for others the debut was just a brief flirtation with the possibility of fame and fortune.

The St. Louis blues scene that Henry Townsend was so much a part of was perhaps best characterized musically by the preponderance of piano-guitar duos. A tense, hard-edge guitar sound played off a sparse piano accompaniment, often with a vocal delivery to match. Henry Townsend's collaborations with the pianist Walter Davis typify the often somber sound that perhaps more than anything is the distinguishing feature of the pre–World War II blues of St. Louis.

Despite the distinctive sounds coming from the St. Louis area, many of these blues artists are now just names on obscure records. Even those like Charley Jordan, an artist with recognition and numerous sessions to his credit, are still biographical enigmas and are destined to remain so. Had the artists traveled more, acquired agents, and played prominent jobs they might have met with greater renown. In the 1920s the Booker Washington Theatre booked famous acts on a weekly basis, like Bessie Smith and Butterbeans and Susie, but with the exception of Lonnie Johnson and Irene Scruggs, very few local blues artists appeared there.

The St. Louis blues community could not even depend on support from the local press. Beginning around 1912 St. Louis had its own black newspaper, the *St. Louis Argus*. Published weekly, the *Argus* was operated by middle-class blacks who viewed blues music and its musicians with disdain. To these arbiters of taste, jazz was on the borderline of respectability; blues most definitely was disreputable. Outside of occasional advertisements, the names of Roosevelt Sykes and Walter Davis, even though they made hundreds of records, fail to appear in the pages of the *Argus* even once.

Thanks to a chance conversation with Henry Townsend, at least his story can be told in his own words. I had spoken with Henry on several occasions and had read most of his published interviews, but one night in 1986, while we were returning to St. Louis from Chicago, he was in a relaxed mood and reminisced easily about his youth and early days in St. Louis. I soon realized that much of what Henry related was completely new to me, turning much of what I thought I knew on its head. I had never heard stories about Henry's life outside of the music profession. These periods and many other important social aspects of life in St. Louis — racism, police harassment, and bootlegging activities — form the backdrop for the music he produced.

Henry dispelled many myths, especially those surrounding his close friend Walter Davis. That Walter Davis was somehow forced to seek work outside of the music profession has often been lamented. Because he was a desk clerk in a St. Louis hotel, fans and scholars mistakenly assumed that Davis would rather have led the life of a professional musician. Henry Townsend relates, quite succinctly, just why Davis stayed out of music. This and other personal details of Davis's life will necessitate a major rewrite of his biography.

The narrative of this book is drawn from over thirty hours of tape-recorded interviews with Henry Townsend. I have edited them into a chronological story of his life, provided notes and bibliographical references to clarify and augment points Henry raised, and compiled a discography of Henry's recordings. Listening to these fascinating stories unfold was a great pleasure. However, it also brought the sad realization that research into the early days of blues music in St. Louis is now virtually impossible. It is simply too late to speak with the people who lived it. It would have been wonderful to interview others for this project. We did check on some, like Walter Davis's widow, Rose, but we found only Pete Bogans, a guitar-playing friend from the twenties. In addition to Henry, Bogans had played with Pinetop and Milton Sparks, their sister Jimmie Lee, and the trombone player Ike Rogers. Although he did supply us with some information — helping to trigger Henry's memory on a couple of occasions — he was not as helpful or as forthcoming as we both had hoped. Unfortunately, Pete Bogans died in 1990, leaving Henry as the last remaining St. Louis bluesman of the era.

In many respects St. Louis has been sadly neglected by blues researchers — seemingly always taking a backseat to Chicago and Mississippi. The little knowledge we do possess only serves to illuminate how much we missed. I hope that Henry Townsend's story will help redress the balance somewhat and will spur other researchers to find equally compelling tales of vintage St. Louis blues players.

a blues life

"LIKE A BULLET"

Shelby, Mississippi, is where we originated from. My grandparents had a farm in Shelby; they owned, I guess, 180 acres down there. My grandfather was named Lazarus Blunt and my grandmother was named Annie Blunt.

My father's name was Allen and my mother's name was Amelia — of course the Townsend stands. Her name was Blunt before she was wedded to my father. My mother was born right there in Shelby; my father was born a little way out at a little place called Sunflower, Mississippi. I was born October 27, 1909, in Shelby. Shelby is not too far below Clarksdale — it's approximately one hundred miles out of Memphis.

I never got a chance to meet my father's parents and I only got to see two of his brothers — I think it was his baby brother named Luke, and I got a chance to see one that I'm named after, Jesse. And the other one I never got to see, his name was James. I got a chance to see one of my father's sisters, and I slightly recall that because I saw her in Mississippi. But that's a kinda faded thing, but I can remember her. I remember she bought me a glass pistol with little red candy balls in it — that was something to make me remember her, you know.

I really don't know what my father's parents done for a living. My father was kind of a strange man. He was very quiet and I never knew him to seek after his relatives or anything. Now he had one brother, his baby brother — he would find him and visit him no matter where he go, and he was a peculiar guy too. He never rode a train or rode a car or wagon or anything. Wherever he went, he walked. And he would visit my dad, I don't care how far he moved. He moved from Shelby to Lula, which is a long ways. Didn't matter to him, he walked to see him. And when my dad had moved other places, he'd get one visit and he'd walk.

When my father left Shelby, he purchased about forty acres of land in Lula, but unfortunately for us the land went up under water, so it wasn't too much a success. Just about the year we were there was the year that the water come. Then the next year the water come and re-peated itself. So he see that wasn't gonna do too well, so he got rid of that.

We moved from Lula, Mississippi, to Memphis. We was only in Memphis a couple of months. I must have been about six years old at the time. I had started school when I was in Mississippi, but just that one part of the school session, the end of the school session. We moved out of there then, and I went to school the couple of months we was in Memphis. My father didn't do anything while we were in Memphis; he seeked out work but he never did find none. So he decided then to bring the family over to Caruthersville, Missouri. I have two brothers which was with us in Mississippi, but they didn't travel with us when we started traveling; they stayed at home there with my grandparents. I was the only one that traveled with my parents, just me. And we came over to Caruthersville, Missouri, and he kinda hired himself out to a cotton compress company there, and he worked for them a while. And I was in school there for a short period of time. We was there about a year, maybe two years, I guess. I must have been about seven years old — something like that — when we was in Caruthersville.

Now the year that we was in Caruthersville my grandfather sold his property in Mississippi. He bought property in Cairo, Illinois, and moved to Cairo. And about that time my parents were just about ready to leave Caruthersville. I think the army worms came through there and kinda cleaned things up — didn't leave much farm work because they just kinda ruined the cotton crop and everything else. We called them army worms: today they're in this crop, tomorrow they would be in another crop, and just like that. They would just destroy crops as they go along. So we left there that year and come to Cairo. And we stayed there with my grandfather a month or two, just about a couple of months. This was my mother's father.

We didn't stay with him too long, and we come to the city. We lived in Cairo for a brief moment, then my father seeked another piece of property out there in Miller City — it's right out from Cairo, about twelve miles out from Cairo. He got a place out there and worked that farm out there. Then we left Miller City and come back down to Cairo to my grandfather's place.

My brothers had both come over to Cairo with my grandfather. The one that's just older than me was named Charley and the other one was named Lazarus. We was all living there with my grandfather then. Matter of fact, they called it the big house. And my grandfather built enough room for all of his children, and he had at that time three daughters that were alive. The baby daughter died before he left Mississippi. He built it so his daughters and their family could be there. It was a big house, like I said. Not the penitentiary Big House, but a farm big house.

My grandfather was a self-educated man. I didn't have too much school, but he didn't have any at all — but he was educated. He educated himself, and he gave himself a real good education. After he come to Cairo he deposited quite a bit of money there — enough money for them to be interested in him becoming a member of the bank board. And he was president of the bank for a while. Well, he had the most money in there, so they weren't scared of him stealing it!

He had a huge farm and had people working, just like the plantation type thing. He was farming cotton, corn, wheat, and fruits — he had a little bit of all of it. I can recall that orchard — the season come around for those apples, plums, and peaches to get ripe, I couldn't wait to get out there. I recall that.

My brother Lazarus and my cousin, which is my mother's sister's kid — my grandfather built them a house on the property not too far from the main house. My mother's sister's husband, he was kinda in the bootlegging business. His name was Dave Williams. My mother's sister's name was Irene Williams. Somehow or another somebody beat Dave Williams for his still, stole his distillery. He didn't know who got it, and he thought that it was my older brother Lazarus and his own stepson, which his name was Ike and was born to Irene Williams before Dave married her. So he thought they stole the distillery. So he wanted revenge now. So what he done was, he come up to the house where my dad and all of them was and he told us, said, "Well if don't nobody tell me where that distillery is, I'm gonna burn both of these houses down." So my father told him, "No, don't burn the houses down. Maybe we can get things worked out. Maybe we can get hold to another still if you don't find that one, because I wouldn't want you to burn the house down for a whiskey still."

So he was one of these hot-headed fellows, and he insisted he was gonna do that. So sure enough, he went out to the little town and bought him some coal oil and came back and burned the house down where my brother and them lived. Then he went back to town to get some more coal oil — he was gonna burn the house down where we were staying. And my grandfather — he was a pretty old man at that time — he and my daddy begged him not to do that. But of course he insisted on doing it. And when he started at the house with the coal oil, my daddy asked him to go back, and he wouldn't go back, so my daddy killed him. He shot him. My daddy moved away from there after he come clear of it. It wasn't nothing done about it because all the witnesses said it was in defense — no charges.

Lazarus was living with some girl down there. He was a teenager himself, because that was real early. I was a kid, I guess close to eight years old. I'd been going to school out there in Klondykes — that's a little village out there about five or six miles out from Cairo. That's where we went to school at, because at this time I was living between Cairo and this little Klondykes place. I have never lived in Future City. That's something that has to be totally ignored.[1] Ike, the stepson of Dave Williams, his family lived in Future City. I was living in St. Louis when I knew anything about Future City too much, because I'd go back down there and I'd stop at his place. Future City is not in the makings for me, really. Before I came to St. Louis I didn't know anything about Future City at all.

We were living in Miller City when I first heard this guitar sound. My father met a friend over there — an associate of his — I think his

name was Will Davis, but they called him Otto, and he played a guitar. I was in bed at night and he and my dad would get making them
sounds. My dad played an accordion. That's when I heard the thing
that really tore my mind up for the guitar. The sound of that guitar
just went through me, just penetrated me like a bullet. That was my
first real inspiration. I knew what I liked from that point on. I knew
then that I wanted to play a guitar. Otto was playing the reels on the
guitar, and he was a pretty good little guitar player. Matter of fact, Otto
came to St. Louis — getting a little advanced of what I'm speaking
about — but he came to St. Louis after I started playing. I got a chance
to be with him a little some. He was the first guitar player that I remember in person to see playing. The very first.

My dad did not really play guitar. He could do a lick or two on
guitar, but he played an accordion. He played blues something like
Clifton Chenier — it was somewhat his style. He wasn't that great, but
he played, I can say that. He never did reach a peak like that, because
he just done it for his entertainment, and that was all. I don't know
where he learned to play it at, because he was playing it when I come
in knowledge of it. I guess he must've had it all the time, because I
don't remember when he got the accordion or anything like that.
When I remember he was playing, and the first time I kinda remember him playing was in Caruthersville.

Some of the same old songs you hear now — "Hurry Sundown See
What Tomorrow Brings" — that was one of my dad's songs then. I hear
songs now that people think is new with words created by so-and-so.
God knows where the words come from, because way before my time
I heard it, and people's doing it now. But back then that word wasn't
used, *blues*. I never heard that word used. They called them reels back
then. You'd get scolded about singing one of them. Ungodly songs.
Most of us wasn't allowed to do that. My grandparents' — you couldn't
do it there. My daddy didn't bother about it, but my grandparents' —
you couldn't do it. But we'd do it.

The time where my brother Charley and I was together in Cairo,
he and I would go to the ten-cent store and buy us a harp when we
got hold to a quarter or something. We'd buy us a ten-cent harp and
each of us learned to blow harps. And we done a little entertaining

with those harps. He learned to blow real good, and I learned to blow good enough. I guess I was about as good as Robert Nighthawk was on harp, something like that. We entertained a little bit around town, around Cairo down there. Little parties and whatnot — we had a dual harp thing.

We didn't play on street corners. It wasn't permitted, because I was much too young to be doing what I was doing. To get out where everybody could see it, that would have got me in trouble. So what we'd do is put the harps in our pockets, and when we'd get the chance to go and visit somebody, then we'd slip off to little parties. And we'd done parties for adults, but we kept everything in perspective, because if the parents would've got hold to it, at our age, then it wouldn't have worked. But speaking about that guitar sound and the music sound, this is where I got the idea, from Will Davis — Otto, as we called him. He is the one what give me the inspiration for the idea that I just had to play guitar.

Then I got myself into a little jam about blowing snuff into my cousin's eyes. He lives in Chicago now. His name is Benjamin Henderson — my mother's baby sister's child. I was slightly older than him. And so my daddy was gonna get me for that, and that's when I first left home. You don't know how bad it hurts my feelings for me to think that somebody is gonna physically interfere with me, like hitting on me. You don't know how bad it hurts me. My heart jumps and tears in two like busting a string. I can't stand that. I don't dish it out and I can't stand it. I've been whipped but it wasn't a pleasant thing for the man that whipped me — or me — I'll tell you that.

What happened was this. I had worked that week. There was a road building contracting company coming through there, and I had worked for them, and I think I had made about eight or twelve dollars, something like that. And I was allowed to go to town and do my own shopping. I had bought me a new pair of pants — dress pants — and a nice shirt and that's about it. And I had maybe two or three dollars left. You could buy a pair of pants for two and a half dollars, cheap pair for one and a half dollars, and a shirt could cost you ninety-eight cents. That's what I wore away from there, because that's what I had on when I committed the act.

I blowed that snuff in my cousin's eyes and my daddy told me, "Well, I'm gonna whip ya." And he didn't get to me that minute, so I didn't give him no chance. I caught the train. I didn't know where I was going — I didn't care. I knew I wasn't gonna stay there and get a whooping.

I was just about nine years old, somewhere in that neighborhood. I kind of think I was, to the best of my recollections, because I don't remember acknowledging to myself a birthday soon after I got to St. Louis. The next birthday I remember, I was age ten, and I hadn't been here no whole year. So I would say I was just about nine. I come straight to St. Louis. I came up on the railroad, which my father's farm was just west of the railroad. I walked up on that railroad and I caught the Illinois Central. It was going someplace. If it had been turned the other way, it would have been just as well.

The train slowed down in other towns and other places. I think it did stop somewhere, but there wasn't no city lights or no nothing. And it stopped and done some switching, but I didn't see nothing out there but them people waving them lights and things, 'cause it had got dark. I got off in the yard over there in East St. Louis. I didn't get off like experienced hoboes would do. I rode on down in the yard and was fortunate enough to get by and nobody bothered me. I was supposed to get off way back up the line in that little old town just before you get to East St. Louis.

After I got to St. Louis I didn't try to contact my parents. I didn't want to contact them — I didn't know the consequences. So I figured, "Well, whatever is whatever. I'll suffer the consequences." I've always heard that if you make your bed hard, you've got to lay on it. And I kinda remembered that, so whatever I done was my fault. But I can't ever recall in my mind that I ever wish that I hadn't left. I hear most people say, "Oh, I left home and I wish that I had never." I ain't never wished that. I guess that I got along pretty good.

I remember when I arrived in St. Louis it was the summertime. I remember more or less all the events. I arrived here in the middle of the week — it must have been about Wednesday, the exact date I don't know. Two days I called myself looking for work. One day not look-ing for work and going to somebody's house. The next day nobody looked for work, so that put that day to be a Sunday. Now I remember that distinct because I was a bit curious and excited over being away from home, and each detail was important to me. What was I gonna do next? What the next move would be — you know, survival.

I had two or three dollars. Stopping in one of them restaurants buying a brain sandwich or something like that for a dime or so, I knew that wasn't gonna last me too long. I slept out the first two nights. It's kinda faint to me now — since they tore Market Street down, I can't quite place where it was — but if the buildings were still there, I could tell you exactly the spot where I slept. The third night I met these two fellows. One we called Blue. The other guy, his name was Earl Keys. He was a nephew to this famous black doctor that used to be in St. Louis, Dr. Keys. So then I started hanging in with them.

One of them was cleaning up a theater, a little old theater that used to be on Market Street. We used to call it Funky London. It was a little old show, a little nasty show. That wasn't what it was named, but that's what most people started to calling it. It was London — that's what the show was named — but we called it Funky London because it was cheap. You could go in there for a nickel sometimes and a dime other times. The kids would play hookey from school and they would go in there and, being kids, they would piss all over in the dark. They just sit in the seat and piss, and you could smell the piss and stuff. They couldn't clean it up good enough. So one of these boys would clean up in there.

Earl never did do much of nothing. I think some of Earl's people would furnish him with a little money and he'd come down there and share with us, buy us little things on occasion. Then we all three started staying with a lady called Eva Watts, and she would make us work, clean up the kitchen, and she kept the house spotless. She had a pretty good size house and we had to dust, but she was feeding us. This was over on Walnut Street, just east of Jefferson. We would do whatever little chores needed doing around there. She was giving us a whole lot, but I thought then, being as I was working cleaning, I was earning; I didn't understand. Now I know I wasn't earning nothing. She didn't need me to clean up her kitchen. That didn't last long — a couple of weeks at the most. Then I found me a job shining shoes. This was in the first month of being in St. Louis.

Then I got me a job with a very reputable guy — he was a famous man in the city, although he wasn't at that time. His name was E. B. Koonce. He later became an undertaker.[2] He had a shoeshine parlor, which was an alcohol and water joint — a speakeasy, they call it. Shine shoes out front, but in the back we had other things. The shoeshine parlor was on Short Market. Market Street came to Jefferson and continued sightly to the left. Short Market ran right up there to the V and continued on out that way about two blocks and that was it. On the corner used to be a finance company. But that was Short Market right in there. I started shining shoes there, and whatever I made I turned over to the other boy, and he'd cashier for him. Then later on this other fellow quit, so he just told me, "Well, you take it over." He'd come by and check me out, see what I need, polish and stuff.

Whatever I needed he'd go and get it, bring it back, and drop it off. I'd make three dollars, four dollars. That's a whole lot of money in a shoeshine parlor then, because shoeshine was a nickel and a dime. And if you mustered up four or five dollars shining shoes, that's a whole lot of people coming in there. But he wouldn't take no money. He would always say, "Okay, see me next time." I was doing what he wanted me to do, which was to front.

I found out a little later on, after I got a little hip to the deal, that I was a kinda cover-up kid out there working. I didn't mind, because the guy was, well, I wouldn't say they was paying me what it was worth, but I was being compensated so that I could live. I couldn't say that it was a good deal, really, because the truth is the way it was then: if the city law enforcement policemen had've come in and found me there and nothing other than me and any evidence, I'd've gone to jail just like anybody else.

Another thing I used to do was get out and scout and find bottles. Bottles were kinda scarce; half-pints — they were called shorts — and that's what the bootleggers preferred. Even though it was six ounces, he'd call it a half-pint. You got a nickel for the regular half-pint size, but you got a dime for that six ounce half-pint. And that was pretty good, because you could find them. The bootleggers had it in the bottles; you don't have to bring the bottle back, you take it on with you. Now if a guy takes it with him, he throws it away. So you find it and you take it back along with four or six more bottles, and you sell them to the bootlegger. So I used to do that too.

I never did go back to school no more. One of the things that kept me out of school was that I would have been found out. They wouldn't have let me in. And another thing that I don't quite understand is why no truant officer never bothered me. Or bothered those two other kids, because they were kids just like myself. I don't remember ever being questioned by a truant officer. I guess they didn't have no way to come searching for me and no reason to search for me. They didn't have nothing to guide them toward me except, "Here's a kid, I wonder who he is?" So I'm not in the files nowhere. So they probably said, "Well, forget him." Maybe that's what they said.

Right in this time bracket I decided to look for a faster paying job, and I went to Union Station to see if I could get hired there. Those people there had a lot of traffic and they were busy making a lot of money. I was picked up there by policemen and they arrested me. God knows why. They charged me with a joke: of suspecting me of trying to steal the clock out of the tower up there in Union Station! They made a joke out of it. I was really charged with that, but they finally turned me loose. They didn't know whether they turned me loose to a parent or nothing — I wasn't even asked them questions. They just locked me up and held me. I wasn't held overnight, but I was held from in the morning to over in the evening.

From that time on I was a little leery about policemen and all of that. And at the time it kinda done something to me. It made me a little unwilling to deal with the law, to be cooperative with the law, because that was so unjust to me — so unjust. I couldn't understand why they would do that to me. I would understand it now, because now I know what was what. Anyway, I got over that, and I played the game with Koonce for I don't know long, but it was a good long spell — a good year, or it could've been better than that.

I got kinda girl crazy right about there. Well, what else was there for me to do but to get kinda girl crazy? I'm out there, I'm already a man in my own rights, and I know about what's going on the world. Not that I got a hold to any gal or not, but I come to being enthused, you know what I mean. The gals would look at me and say, "Get outta the way, little ole boy." But this hung on until I got old enough for them to look at me and say, "Well, maybe." But it was there, it was there.

Now Blue was a little older than I was. I think both of them was a little older than me, but I was a little larger than Earl. But Blue had a girlfriend, and I think that's what kinda got me interested in it. He and his little girlfriend would get together and they'd be kissing and hugging and going on and I thought, "What's wrong with me? How come I can't?" But didn't nothing work for me then, but like I said, I was into it myself. I was very interested in it — I'll put it that way. But it was a few years before anything started to happen.

After we left Eva's house all three of us got a room. We maintained that room about five or six months and then we split up and each went their own way. I started to work for a fellow called Dave Flowers. I sold whiskey for him, and this is what brought me loose from the room that we all had together.

When I started work with him he had rented a house on Jefferson Avenue, about two or three doors north of Pine Street, and that's where I stayed. I was there day and night — my job didn't end. When I wanted relief I just left and went and done something else and come back and my job was still there. Anytime anybody knocked on the door, I was ready to serve them whatever they want. It was just transit — they come by and go. I was only a kid, about eleven or twelve years old at this time.

Dave Flowers was a great politician and he was very popular then. Dave Flowers had a reputation, but didn't nobody bootleg any more than a fellow called Jordan Chambers. Jordan Chambers was also a great politician and he was a bootlegger and he had joints and things. It's just like the politicians now, but back then there wasn't anybody to bother Jordan Chambers because he was too powerful. Back then whatever Jordan Chambers said do, believe it or not, the city done it. Officials done it because he was powerful enough to pull them out.[3]

Jordan Chambers also started something like baskets of food for people at Christmas. He was in the undertaking business at first, and he wasn't as strong politically as he was later on. I think the bootleg-ging and the undertaking all kinda paralleled, it all went side by side. And I don't really know when or if he ever got out of it. He was on top of the square side. Just political power is what he seeked out, and that's what he gained.

Now Dave Flowers may have been a kinda hoodlum, I don't know. He appeared to be, because a lot of people kinda feared Dave for some reason. There was such a thing that existed then as black gangsters — the Mafia type blacks that made things go certain ways. They never was no big historical thing, but they existed.

I must have worked for Dave Flowers a year or so, maybe a year and a half. Being who he was and on top of things as a politician, I never had no trouble. Nobody never come in. Now I wouldn't doubt that even I had sold to a policeman — I wouldn't doubt that at all. But there was nothing ever said and nobody ever questioned me about anything. I never was busted or arrested or anything.

Now, I do not recall the reason why I was no longer working for Dave. I must have moved onto something different and I don't recall what it was. I think I went to my brother's and started staying. My older brother Lazarus had moved away from home and was out for his self, and he was living over on Biddle Street about the 1800 block. I may've went to his house, because there was a time when I did stay with him. I used to steal all his clothes and wear them away. I could wear his shoes, but his other stuff — well, he was tall. I would go over and borrow his shoes when he didn't know it. This was two or three years before I went into music, and also I'd gone back to riding freight trains then.

That's when I started going back home, back down to Cairo. By this time my parents were here in St. Louis, but after they got here I started to visiting back down there. I'd go down to Future City. My grandpar-ents were still there, and this cousin of mine — the snuff in the eye — he was still in Cairo. Him and I were about the same age. He was a little closer to me than my own brothers were because I was around him more. So I would go back and see him and my grandparents. And I'd also go out to Future City — my other cousin and his family lived out there. But I don't believe I ever spent a night in Future City.

My parents knew where I was about a year and a half after I was in St. Louis. They moved to St. Louis, but I didn't go back home, and they didn't try and tell me to go back. They tried to talk to me, to put me in school, but I felt that I was too far behind. I'd been making it on my own and, being a kid, I didn't realize they were telling me the best thing. I kept promising them that I was gonna do it, and after a while they quit pressuring me about it.

The last place I went to school at was the Klondykes, out from Cairo. And at the end of that season I would have graduated to the fourth grade. I was in the third. I was always behind because of the migrating my parents were doing, from one town to another. And that's bad on a kid, very bad. So that had me slightly behind then. And after these years had expired, I didn't feel that I wanted to go back into school, because I knew what would happen. The other kids would have harassed me, teased me about being x amount of age and in the baby grades and all that. But I wasn't qualified to do anything else.

After I realized that I wasn't going to go back to school and that it wasn't going to be feasible for me to go back after a period of time, I started to take on some of the things in life that I needed to know for my own self. To learn to read and write and understand the meanings of words. I guess I got some of that from my grandfather. I went to work on that myself. I took it upon myself to see what I could do about it. I've always wanted to know much more than I guess I could ever know, and I've worked for it. I haven't come out of school yet, my school. So I done good, I think. And regrets — I've never had any, really. So after my parents realized that I wasn't willing to go back, they just relaxed on me and give me a full swing: "Whatever you want to do." My mother told me, "Whatever you do, remember there's a God. Ask him to be with you, whatever it is." And I've always remembered that, no matter what it was that I was not able to do — anything by myself that I needed help with. Some people take it for granted: "Oh, you're gonna get that." Maybe yes and maybe no, who knows? Faith in yourself is good, but I don't think it's nothing wrong if you believe in the supreme power. Have faith in that too. I think it helps.

But I came through it. It was a crisis, but I didn't understand it as such because a kid like me didn't have any business being away from home. I had two parents and between me and my two parents was just a spanking. Now I shouldn't have been away from home, as you know, but an individual is an individual, and that's where it's at. If I'd have been one of my other brothers I'd have been at home, but I wasn't.

What I done would be impossible to do now because the age is different. At that time people as a whole, no matter what condition they were living under, they still had some respect for children. Even if you went outside your own race, there was some respect for a child. Nowadays you can forget that. They don't have no respect for the child or the child's parents or nobody else. If you don't respect yourself, there ain't no respect for you. So I wouldn't think no kid, no nine years old, could get out here now and do nothing except if somebody take him in or take him to the juvenile.

The East St. Louis riots happened before I came to St. Louis, but that was still a fresh thing, it hadn't cooled off.[4] And the worst part of it, it was beginning to spread over to St. Louis. It was a lot of tension. When the riot came about, there were more blacks armed than was thought to be. And the whites suffered a whole lot more casualties than the blacks did at first.

East St. Louis was a major migration area for people from the South. And everybody out of the South had a .45 or a .38 or something, and that was underestimated among the whites over there that got this thing kicked off. And the blacks actually slaughtered them people over there.

Now it wasn't too long after the riot that I came to St. Louis — two years at the most. Being a nine-year-old kid, I still knew what was happening. I had to know because I'm still here and I observed what was happening. Those white people were slaughtered, and when they did send in the state troopers to stop the riot, that's when the most blacks was killed.

The state troopers killed more blacks than the rioters. The state troopers came down and put the number up higher among the blacks. If they hadn't've come down and done that, you could've said the minimum amount of blacks would have died. They had to say blacks were slaughtered by the whites or this would be saying the governor of Illinois killed people instead of the rioters. So they said more blacks were killed than whites.

* * *

In St. Louis at the time, Market and Chestnut Streets were strictly red light, as they call it. Everything happened in this section — you name it and it was there, anything you wanted. In that particular part of town — Market, Chestnut, Walnut Streets — it was noted for prostitute houses. The girls would sit in the windows as you pass by and they'd peck on the window, "Come in," and all that.

The red light area was sectioned off, like on Chestnut Street, which is east of Lawton. Lawton was an extension of Chestnut. Chestnut Street was red light district all the way downtown where there was dwelling houses — Market Street to around Twenty-third and Market, on the north side of the street. Right there at that little ole show we used to call Funky London, from there back up was all red light district. Gals would be knocking on the windows in there. Twenty-second Street, Beaumont and Franklin, on Beaumont going back south — all that row of flats there was all red light. You could go in there and get anything you wanted to get. Visit the doctor for fifty years! Anything you want. All that come free — you pay for the body. It was strictly in and out. Transit, real fast transit. Fast as them gals could get rid of it. It was just like fast food, put in your order, pay and go.

Believe it or not, that kind of carrying on supported the economy among the black people pretty well, because it was a whole lot whites would come down and bring the money. And the money would stay in circulation for a while in the black community until it had to go back out and be spent. And it really helped a lot. Most of them gals had pimps, and in turn they would put the money in circulation. It was a bad thing, but good is not always survival. I haven't heard nobody say just what I'm saying, but even then I was wise enough to know it was a great support. It meant something to everybody that was in that settlement.

It was mainly black women there. Occasionally you'd find a few other nationalities down there, because the business was so good. There was a railroad station there, and some of those girls actually had regular customers. There was no entertainment going on in those places, only in the clubs or house parties.

Now there were parties that went on all day and all night in homes. They weren't considered clubs — it was just a speakeasy place where people would go to drink — and this went on continually. Like this place I got here now, this would be an ideal place for it. People would come at all times. The table would have an oilcloth on it so that the waste whiskey wouldn't ruin it. You'd be sitting around there just like a bar or something drinking.

Some of them places was controlled — *run* or *managed* would be the proper word — by blacks. But most of them would belong to Italians. But being in a black neighborhood, they preferred black people to run it. They was fronting, just like I was doing for that speakeasy.

Numbers games were also one of the great things for underprivileged people. There were those games back in the twenties and thirties, where people survived with nickels and dimes. A certain way you could spend a nickel and it could bring you five dollars. All those pennies. The Italians moved in on it when they found out how much money there was to be made off numbers. I played, but I never was too much of a gambler, anyway you start at it. I would play occasionally, and I guess I would consider myself pretty lucky, because most times I played, if I wasn't lucky this time I'd continue to play and get lucky, then come way out ahead and quit. That's the way I kinda operated. I always did feel like I didn't want to be the part of the game that supported it. I wanted to be the guy that got mine and got out again.

When I first got to St. Louis I didn't have no contact with any musicians. When I first started shining shoes over there on Short Market I heard about a lot of musicians, but I never had a chance to see any of them. Where they would be at, I was too young to be permitted to get into those places. My first chance to see any musicians was at the Booker Washington Theatre. The Booker Washington Theatre — that was *it* then. It was a great place, and I found ways that I could sneak in there.

I couldn't go in — they wasn't going to allow that — but I could get in the back and sneak in — get backstage or something like that — and that's when I'd get a chance to see these people. I could hear it out there, but I couldn't go out there where the entertainment was going at. And by this boy Blue working across the street at the London Theater, that made him be acquainted with the people over at the Booker Washington Theatre, and that gave us a little extra chance to sneak in the back, because they would let us. So that's when I first got the chance to see some of the musicians. Ma Rainey, Bessie Smith, and Peg Leg Bates, these are some of the things that I could never forget. That was some excitement for me. This is when they used to book in the famous people of the entertainment world in the Booker Washington Theatre.

The Booker Washington Theatre was located just off Jefferson. Jesse Johnson's record store was at Twenty-second Street, the top of Twenty-second Street, which made him right next door, except for an alley, to the Booker Washington Theatre. I call it an alley, but it was actually Jameston Street; it separated him from the theater. I didn't know hardly anything about Charles Turpin, but he was the guy that managed it — or owned it or what have you.[5]

I remember when Butterbeans and Susie come to that theater. I was a little fellow, but I remember when they come there, but I didn't get the chance to see them. Certain events they screened them pretty good. Because they done some show acts back then that was kinda off-limits for youngsters. What they done is a kinda everyday thing out there in the streets now, but back then you couldn't say "boo" too loud. You had to keep everything in perspective back then, otherwise they would close you up. And there was always somebody there waiting for the wrong thing to happen, making sure there wasn't any underage people in there. And they wasn't doing nothing except what you could see out on the street corner now.

It was customary when any entertainer come in there that there was a vaudeville act with them — a double package. They would be on the road as a show, more than just a vocalist/entertainer. Even if the artist themselves didn't have a package, they would book a package in with them because the length of entertainment would have been far too great for any one vocalist to handle. If they wanted to get quite a bit of money out of it, they would book one of the better vocalists and book one of the great minstrel shows, and that would draw a better ticket.

I had to be twelve or fourteen years old before I was able to go in the theater — a little different than when I was ten or eleven years old. I could kinda sneak in and go to the front after the tickets were sold. But to just go and buy a ticket — I don't think I ever got to that before the Booker Washington Theatre was getting ready to close down.

I saw Lonnie Johnson at the Booker Washington — although by that time he had been all over in East St. Louis, but at that time it wasn't too convenient for me to get to those places. I didn't know nobody that had transportation that was willing to fool with me, and it wasn't like it is now. To get to East St. Louis was a problem unless you want to walk — and I wasn't for that. So my first time of seeing Lonnie Johnson was there. When I first saw him he'd already recorded. I used to sneak in and see him. He also played at a few places where Luella Miller and them got started at — I can't call the street now, but it's a couple of blocks from Market Street. Lonnie Johnson used to be over there and on Twenty-Second Street there, them speakeasy joints and things.

See I could get into them places — it wasn't no problem. I was big enough to get into those places because the other thing was against the law in the first place. So I wasn't violating the law — there wasn't a law to violate. I could go in there, but I couldn't participate in the action, because I was a kid. I could go and sit down, but nobody would give me nothing to drink. But they didn't care as long as I go in and act like a kid. Like if some of my parents was there and I went over and sit down, they didn't care about that. So I got a chance to see Lonnie around quite a bit.

Lonnie Johnson was quite an influence on guitar players all over the world. He hasn't been talked about, in my opinion, as much as he deserves to be. Lonnie was what you'd call the guy that paved the way. He was one of these people. An innovator of guitar pickin', especially the black blues style guitarist. He was to guitar what Sonny Boy was to the harmonica, in my opinion. That's the way I feel about it. The man was great at that time, and there just wasn't anybody that exceeded him.

Now there was Blind Lemon Jefferson and several other different guys — they had their trend and their things that they done and was appreciated. But it wasn't the type of thing that Lonnie Johnson done. See, Lonnie Johnson was more of the gut bucket style blues, and Jefferson and them was sort of a New Orleans style, sort of a ragtime style. Occasionally I'd see Lonnie Johnson around East St. Louis. Several places over there he used to work, like down around Third Street and all down in there.

Now it was great to hear Lonnie Johnson because I was hearing what I like — I wasn't playing no guitar then at all, but that's what I wanted to do so bad — and he was one of the people that made me really want to go into it. And I can't exclude Dave Pearchfield, because even before I left home he come down to Cairo and was playing his guitar. Now that was another buildup that made me want it much more. Then when I got to St. Louis and heard Lonnie Johnson, well I sure enough got a habit now. So that's when I went in to push to get this guitar all the way through.

Dave Pearchfield was the first musician I knew in St. Louis. I knew him from Cairo but he lived in St. Louis, although he had relatives that lived out from Cairo. Now he's the first person that I knew about playing music here in St. Louis. And then from Dave Pearchfield to Son Ryan. And the next would be Dudlow Joe — we called him Blue. His real name was Harry something, and he played guitar. He was employed with this Cerkin moving van — I think they still exist.[6] And he was the next which I hooked up with. He was elder to me but he kind of taken me under his wing, kinda protective, you know.

Dave Pearchfield was one of the greater musicians in the city, but he wasn't entertaining other than by coincidence. Like maybe he's somewhere and he had a guitar and when he played he would draw a crowd. That wasn't planned, it was just a coincidental thing. He had a reputation of being a great musician, but he never did use his gift of talent to do anything for anybody like entertaining. But as soon as I got into it I went to using it to benefit something and I got on the street corners. But he didn't do that. Son Ryan played at house parties. Henry Spaulding was diligent about that — he didn't want a weekend to pass him unless he was playing somebody's party.

"THE SWEETEST GUITAR
I'VE EVER PLAYED"

In my teenage years I ran into a little problem with a policeman, or rather two policemen. I don't know their names, but they beat
the hell out of me trying to make me say I knew something about a
man on a junk wagon stealing some batteries. The man's name was
Slick and he was a junker, and he would rent the wagon and horse from
a junkyard.

He was coming down Easton Avenue on his wagon. I knew him,
and when I saw him I jumped up on the wagon with him and rode
down to the junkyard. Well now, he detected an old T Model Ford
following him, and it was the police. So he knew more about what was
going on than I did. So this little pony he had was fast, and he called
the pony to get on down there. And I'm on the wagon with him and
I don't know what is what. And he actually beat that T Model Ford
down to the junkyard with that horse.

He got off there and took the batteries off and he'd told the Jew
when he drove in, "hot stuff." Well them Jews were buying it, and they
stripped them batteries off there and put them in the basement right
away. When the police came on up there they didn't get no evidence,
but they arrested this man and me, and we went to jail.

They separated us, as usual. They put him somewhere and they
come back trying to butter me up by telling me, "Well, your buddy's
snitchin' on you — he done told it all, how y'all got them batteries."

Well, I know that's a damn lie. They didn't know that. I knew it was a lie; they was fishing. I wouldn't come across with nothing, because I didn't know nothing.

They tried to make me sign this paper there. "Put your X on that." They didn't know whether I could write or not. This nigger, I guess he can't write, just put his X on that! So I refused, and one of them slapped me upside the head. "Put it on there!" Called me the name. Pow! Had my head going.

So now I saw my chance. I said, "Okay, okay." Now I know I can't do none of these two here, but this guy sitting over there is gonna make them do something to me bad. I eased over. They done relaxed now because they just know I'm fitting to sign that thing. And they used to have them great big old inkwells that used to sit there, and I got that inkwell and aimed it and got him right in the head. Boy, I tried to tear his head open, and I did. I cut a hell of a hole in his head.

But by this time I don't know nothing. Shit, they done put me to sleep right away. So three days later I woke up in Number Two.[1] Boy, my head felt as big as a television set. So you know what? They didn't do nothing about it, and of course there wasn't nothing I could do. I guess they didn't want to bring it up because they done all of this with no evidence. And I dropped it — I was just glad to get out from under that junk.[2]

About six or eight months later I'm coming up Biddle Street with my guitar in my hand and they was riding this time in a Nash, an old turn car Nash with the top down on it. He pulls up to the curb and says to me, "Get your hands up, nigger, get your hands up." Now I've got my guitar under my arm, so I just raised this one hand.

So the other one driving the car was the same policeman that I'd hit. So he said again, "Get your hands up nigger and drop that guitar." I said no. And this other guy looked out of there and saw me, he said, "Hey, let that black son of a bitch alone or you'll have him to kill."

Anyway, he turned around and got back in the car, and they drove on off. He was the one that I'd hit; I'd've thought he'd been glad to get to me, but he didn't. He said, "You'll have him to kill," and he was right. They would see me periodically, but they never would bother me no more in that particular district.

✳ ✳ ✳

Sometime in 1927 my father had got me a job. It used to be some people name Warschosky who used to have a refining and rubber plant — automobile rubber plant — and it was located down on the river, on one of those streets somewhere near North Market. They used to take old tires, split them, and take the beads out — split the tires and make inner boots out of them.

See, I'd got halfway slick by then: I knew how to live without doing too much of anything. Anyway, I went to work down there where my dad was — he was a foreman there. I'd visited the house a little bit too often and he told me he a had a job for me and I couldn't very well say no. It was in 1927, because that's when the storm came through St. Louis.

I worked down there approximately a month, and one morning he and I was on our way to work, we were walking. We were living at 2014 Carr Street at the time. Anyway, as we were on our way to the job, I lagged behind because I was having brainstorms. I wasn't too particular about the job, and I was having brainstorms about whether I should go to work or not, and it led me right across the river to the railroad. And that's where I went instead of going to work that morning. I don't know what date that was, but it was the same day the cyclone hit.[3] And as I said, the brainstorms that I was having had me headed to Memphis — that's where I was going, just like that. I just walked away from home going to work, in just the clothes what I had on, and I changed my mind and went on and got the train.

I caught the train out of East St. Louis. A little further down there was a place that used to be called Firework Station. I went down that way and caught the train. I climbed to the top. I was gonna ride out in the open air, but it commenced to getting cloudy that morning and all of a sudden it got darker and darker. So I just walked down the train and found me a refrigerator car, opened one of those hatches and pulled the lock down in with me so I couldn't get locked in, and went down in the hatch. If the railroad man had any reason to come by, he would have to open it to get the thing that you lock it with back out. I would know to holler before he got me closed in.

Forty-five minutes or an hour after I got out of the rain, lightnin' was playing around down in there just like I was standing outdoors. I could hear the wind and I could hear all these sounds, and it went on for quite a spell. I don't know where or when I went to sleep at, but I do know I didn't arrive in Memphis before the next morning. I hadn't caught the train out until about noon, and it had stopped somewhere. I was headed to Memphis but I didn't care — I knew it was going to get there sooner or later. If it had went on by Memphis I wouldn't have cared — down in Mississippi somewhere, it wouldn't have made me no difference. As I always say, I can't be lost because I don't know where I'm at in the beginning!

Anyway, the train got to Memphis and pulled down in the yard. They had a pretty rough man down there then, and I think they called this guy Winchester Pete. There was two of them there, one called Leadbelly and one called Winchester Pete, and Winchester Pete was a brutal man when it come to blacks. He got fun out of shooting them in his railroad, as he called it. I think that this is the right names; I hope I don't get these name confused because I rode in so many yards I might get some of the railroad detectives' names confused. I know that he was one of the cruelest people when it comes to blacks.

But before I got off the train I heard a newsboy: "Read all about it, St. Louis Cyclone." I said, "What!" This kinda disturbed me right quick. So I listened closely to what he was saying, and I'm thinking about all my people there.

By that time this officer of the railroad said, "Hey boy!"

I don't know where he come from. I said, "Yes sir?"

"Where you going?"

I said, "I'm going back to St. Louis now."

He said, "No you ain't, you not gonna catch no train in here."

I said, "Well I'm sorry to say it, I may not make it out but I'm gonna sure try."

He said, "What do you mean telling me you're gonna try?"

I said, "Look, all of my people is in St. Louis and I just left there yesterday. They may or may not be dead but I don't have no way to get back there but riding one of these trains."

He looked at me for a second or two, then said, "Okay, I'm gonna tell you what you do. You ain't gonna catch no train here. See that water tower up there? You light out of here walking now, you can get a train out of here in the next thirty minutes. You got about fifteen minutes to get to that water tower. Get on the other side of the water tower before you get on the train. I'm gonna ride it that far, and if you waits on it before then and I see you, I'm gonna shoot you."

I told him okay because I know that wasn't no problem. I walked on up there to the water tower and I didn't get hardly nowhere on the other side before the train was coming on out. Now it was pretty hot though — it was hotter than I'd expected. I think he kinda told them people to get up as much steam as they could so I couldn't get on. And it come out of there double puffing. But when it got there I got it. I didn't have no choice — I was gonna ride. It would hardly go too fast for me. So I caught the train and come back to St. Louis. I was pretty much disturbed.

I reached the city, I guess sometime that evening, and got off the train in East St. Louis and commenced thumbing, trying to get a ride over to St. Louis. I finally got a ride and everybody was well. They was worried to death about me. So we all hugged and got pacified and what have you. I stayed home then for somewhat better than a month. But I didn't go back to the job.

The cyclone didn't get downtown. It came down Enright, Delmar, Cook Avenue, and Morgan Street and all up in there, in the 4100 block, 4200 and 4300 block.[4] It just swept right across, just made a path. It took roofs off houses leaving people in the bed. It took people, bed, mattress, and all and set them in the streets. This was told to me by reliable people, because I wasn't there. I saw some of the houses where the roof was took off, furniture just sitting in the house like it always was. Lonnie Johnson made a record about that.[5] I know it certainly turned dark, really dark. They say it turned like night here in the city of St. Louis.

✳ ✳ ✳

It took me a long time to try and figure out how I was gonna get me a guitar. I didn't know how, when, or where, but I knew sooner or later I'd get one. They didn't cost that much, but any amount was a great amount at that time. Anyway, it was while I was working with my dad at that plant that I met the lady who bought me my first guitar.

Her name was Corrine and she bought the guitar at Sam Wolff's music store at Jefferson and Franklin. Sam Wolff had two stores by then, he had one on Thirteenth Street[6] and he had this place up there too. Joe's Music bought that place from Sam — it ain't there no more.[7] It was a pretty guitar too, a Stella, good guitar. It could have cost between fifteen and twenty dollars, and that was a whole lot of money for a guitar. You'd get guitars between four and six dollars.

I'd had the chance to bang on other people's guitars, and I began to learn a little something, but you know how often that could happen. I think it took her a couple of months to get it; she put it in the will-call and finally paid it out. She wanted to give me everything that she could afford and I got tired of saying no, so I let her.

That guitar and me worked together for, I don't know, a good spell, a long time. And this is the stupid part: I wasn't getting it out of the guitar as fast as I wanted to and — I guess you've heard people say this a thousand times — I took it out on the guitar. I worked at it and I never could get that guitar to respond like I wanted it to respond. And I just caught a hold to the neck of it and put it to rest. I tore the guitar up.

Now a couple of days later I want me another guitar — this is how the minds of young foolish people can be! Ambition pushes you over a cliff. Then I had to go to work myself and try and find me a guitar. I found me a Thorn or a Thornton — I ain't heard of the name before or since — the sweetest guitar I've ever played in my life. I think I paid a dollar and a half for it in peach shape. I got it out of a pawn shop. Somebody must have made that guitar, but whoever he was he knew what he was doing. So I didn't tear that one up — that one got stole from me. I held onto it for a number of years.

I was going to these places myself and I'd see Dave Pearchfield quite often. And at certain intervals I'd see Son Ryan. But now David had got me kicked off to playing a couple of little sounds that indicate to me that I would learn to play guitar someday. It wasn't anything that I was really playing, but I had some zeal on the guitar. And my friend Pete Bogans, he had him one piece he could play, and I knew how to tune my guitar so that they would be in harmony together. He kinda played the bass part of the guitar and I would frequent the little bit I know down at the low end. And it sounded reasonable. At least it was our own genius ideas. We'd be doing our little bits of entertaining down at these house parties. No money, but a hell of a lot of fun. Excitement for people to come and hear what you're doing — that's a big deal when you're getting started in life. It wasn't but one or two things I could do. I'd do this until it sounds like it's gonna sound bad, then I'd do the other thing. That's all I knew to do, but that was enough. I'd sing and play that. These are the things we entertained with. Now I kinda swapped off with Pete Bogans when I met him. He could play a bass and I put mine with it and we had a band there. The good part about it, we learned to do that properly; we wasn't crossin' out one another, we was staying synchronized, and it worked.

As time went on I got with a guy named Harry and he advanced me up to his point, which wasn't a hell of a lot further but added over to what I know; it made a hell of a lot of difference. Then I picked up a little bit of stuff from Son Ryan, but I could never use that with Pete because I didn't know enough about it to make it sound good by itself. And Pete didn't know how to make it fit with what he was doing, the licks was so much different.

That "Cairo Blues" thing that Son Ryan had, I had to add to that going by myself then, and it wasn't too long before I got that "Cairo Blues" together. And I still ain't got no further with it now! Son Ryan was the first person playing "Cairo Blues," to my knowledge. I heard it was somebody else — a fellow called Martin was supposed to have been the father of it — but Son Ryan was the first person I heard play it. We all got it from Son Ryan, but Henry Spaulding was the guy that recorded it first. The lyrics belonged to Henry — those were his lyrics, he wrote the song. The sound is Son Ryan original. Son Ryan was singing "Cairo," but an entirely different version of it. I think Henry's fitted better than Son Ryan's did; there was more tuning with it.

Henry Spaulding would have been about five or six years older than me, something like that. He didn't make but two sides.[8] I never knew him to do too many other numbers other than his recordings. He had another little number — kind of rhythm stepped-up number — but it wasn't saying too much. He was well respected for those two tunes he played, but that was about his limits.

"Cairo Blues" would be part of what I would call a St. Louis sound, definitely. I don't know of anybody anywhere else that actually plays it other than St. Louis people. But I could reverse it back towards the dates and times when it was played. There's two versions that I could use that would be of that time, other than the one that I use now.

Harry and I worked together periodically. He worked at the moving van company on Twenty-third and Carr at the time. There would be days when certain employees would go out and some would not, depending on how many jobs they had. And if Harry didn't go out, we'd get the guitars and go out and serenade all around everywhere, walk the streets. We had a district we'd like to go in, and we'd head down there because we knew we'd get together with a crowd and get some quarters and dimes, have all the drinks we needed, and have a lot of fun.

We'd head down to Wash Street — it's Cole Street now, but it was called Wash Street then — down Twenty-second, Twenty-third on Wash and all the way down to Seventeenth and Wash. We didn't have no certain houses we'd go. Sometimes we'd go all the way back up Franklin Avenue, Twenty-second and Franklin.[9] It was a row of houses in the back — you'd go through a gangway and there was a row of houses built on the alley like a yard. Store fronts on the floor and a row of houses. And we'd go back in there, which was at one time a pretty good place to go and have fun.

There was a lot of people there, and they loved music and would get together and invite you to come in. They would have parties, drinking, and what have you. But it got a little too radical back there. Sooner or later it got the title "Bucket of Blood." People got to hurtin' one another, shootin' and killing, so then we stayed out of it. We started going down to Ninth Street, around in that way, and that stayed pretty calm. See, back then when a couple of people got hurt in the same place, that place was off-limits to most people — nobody would want to go there. I think up there on Franklin Avenue one got hurt bad and one got killed, so that's why they called that the "Bucket of Blood."

So we didn't go there too much. But we played together, sometimes every day or every other day. I stayed with him a while; he'd come and get me, and he and I would get out there on the street. Harry was in his twenties when I was in my teens; he must have been twenty-seven or twenty-eight years old. I don't know where he was originally from; when I knew him he was here in the city of St. Louis.

I first met Pete Bogans down on Thirteenth Street. Pete was about eighteen years old, somewhere thereabouts, and he had just got married and just got separated.[10] He tells a story about his guitar playing. He said some guy come along pickin' a guitar and took his girl away from him. And he went and got him a guitar and he had to pick that guitar. He went and got the guitar and took her back — out-picked the guy, so he got her back.

Then I went and lost this guitar that I had. Pete and I was down on Ninth Street playing — we played down there all night, just to near day at a house. We were on our way back home and we stopped in the park there for a minute. A police station sat on the corner of Tenth and Carr, and between Carr and Biddle Streets was a park. We got sleepy and went to sleep — you could do that then. But it wasn't quite right then, because somebody still beat me for my guitar. But it was a very unusual thing, very unusual for anybody to do that. You used to be able to just go to sleep, lay something besides you, and when you wake up, it's still there. But this time, I don't know. Pete had a guitar there but only my guitar was taken. But it wasn't too long before I got hold to another guitar.

Anyway, the woman who bought me my first guitar, she got to be jealous. I was a little bit afraid, and as it turned out I was right. I was on Thirteenth Street up in the alley where some houses was — I'd go up there and play a little guitar once in a while. And one day she comes up there and told me, "I told you not to come up here." I said, "So!" And when I said that, she pulled an ice pick. She hit at my body and I caught it, but it went right through my hand and I broke it off. She hit at me about ten times with nothing on the handle — I had it in my hand. I wasn't scared of the hits no more because I had it in there. When she got through hitting I just pulled it on through. Then she started to jump on me, so I backed up and knocked her down, and before she got up, I was gone.

I went to the doctor's and had the hand treated, and that was the end of that episode. It was only skin wounds, and by going straight to the doctor and getting the right shots, it stopped any possibility of things going wrong. But it could have hit them nerves. The ice pick went through the middle finger and out the other side into the base of the thumb. It was all flesh. If it had hit a bone, that would've probably been it. So that was the end of that.

A lady named Lorraine, who was the mother of the boxer Archie Moore, was living in the alley of Thirteenth Street at the time, and that's where I was. She and I was starting to get together. This is where that thing got started. Of course I remained away from Corrine then. I didn't get attached back to her under no circumstances. Ice Pick Mama!

But even before that, there was an incident. You see, Corrine had suspected this. I was asleep in bed one night, and all of a sudden what woke me up was her tears dropping in my face. I didn't make no move, I just laid there and sort of put my arm over on her, and when I did that, she just burst out with crying. I asked her what was the matter, and she didn't tell me too much of nothing. So I was pretending I was concerned about her, what was there to cry about, because I didn't know. And I got up and slipped my pants on, steady talking, not in the act like I was fitting to leave. She was telling me that she didn't think I would do such-and-such a thing, and I was trying to find out what she was talking about. So about the time I slipped on my shoes I see she was getting into a rage, so I got my shirt and come on out the house. That was a scary time for me because I thought about her laying there across me crying, tears falling in my face. That wasn't a good sign at all. And what scared me even worse — later on when that ice pick incident come up. I thought, I could have been laying in the bed with death and didn't know it. I wouldn't've known what was happening — that would have been a great disadvantage for me.

But I wasn't really attached to Lorraine then. I'd been there a couple, three or four times and played the guitar, something like that. We'd take chairs and sit out there and I'd play out there sometimes, and that's what it was all about. Then later years I started living with Lorraine and Archie. I started teaching Archie a little. He wanted to box.[11]

Some years ago I was down at the senior citizens' home on Franklin Avenue.[12] I've been a senior citizen for God knows how long, but I hardly ever go there. I was sitting there, and all of a sudden this woman got up and said, "You don't remember me, do you?"

I said, "No, I sure don't."

She said, "You used to court me."

So I said, "Who are you?"

"I'm Corrine."

I said, "Yeah, I remember you, how can I forget you?" And this was the first time I'd seen her since then. I made that remark, I said, "How can I ever forget?" I know she thought of it. And I thought it was very funny that she had the nerve to come up and say something to me at that. But I'm the fault of letting all these kinda things happen. Number one, I shouldn't have let that guitar been bought. I shouldn't have accepted it.

"REVENGE IS SWEET"

In the 1920s there was prohibition. There wasn't no open places to play in — the city was dry. All you could do was go to a speakeasy and get you some alcohol or something. That's one of the reasons there wasn't no broad entertainment. I don't know if that could be credited as to why some of the musicians that come through here didn't hang in, because the livelihood was limited.

You were also subject to get carried out, go to jail. They'd turn you loose, but it would disturb you. You maybe would have to stay there twelve hours, and nobody would want that. The police would do that periodically: they would come to the house where alcohol and water was being sold and raid the house and take everybody to jail. Huntin' money was what they were really doing. The houseman wasn't gonna let you stay there, because you were one of his customers — you know how that goes.

There was a fellow named Johnny Pegg that lived across the street from my mother on the 1800 block of Carr Street, and every weekend they would have parties. The working-class people would go there to gamble and they would have music there too. Alcohol and water, crap table, and hookers. All this here would be in a package; this is where you could go and get whatever you wanted. Good fun — that's what it was all about.

Things like that were scattered all over the city. You might not know about it, but if you listen real carefully you'd hear somebody say something. This is one of the survival things that people had to resort to in order to maintain a certain level — like keep food on the table — and it was also work for the musicians. There was also a piano in the average one of those places, out of tune or whatnot, keys on out. But it was there, and the piano player learned to do miracles on it, because he didn't have nothing to work with in the first place.

I was at Johnny Pegg's one time playing guitar, and the police pulled the wagon up the house and marched us all out of there. Getting arrested was a pretty common thing at that time. A black man or woman really didn't have to do anything; it was a game for the police. It was sad, but this is the way it was. They would get kicks out of this kind of a thing. When they would arrest you they didn't expect nothing out of you, because most of us didn't have nothing to pay them.

Sometimes you would get arrested on a Saturday night and by eleven or twelve o'clock you were back home. Whoever was in charge of the place might have to give up five or ten dollars to the right person. It was very rare they would raid the same place the same night. If only people knew the real truth about how life was back then with black people — it's more than any book can really explain. I never witnessed no things as drastic as chains or beatings, but there were so many little things that went on that just don't seem like it should have been. Back then it was rough, especially being black. They had fun with you because they could get away with everything.

There was one policeman who when he talked with other policeman he sounded like the rottenest guy in the world, but he wasn't, he was the better guy. His name was Sergeant Callahan, and he would talk a lot of stuff and pretend that he was gonna kill everybody, but he never did nothing to nobody. He'd take his stick and hit all up against the wagon like he's hittin' at you, but he never did hit nobody.

Kinloch, which is out there in the county, was also a pretty good little entertaining town at that time, and it was flourishing. Kinloch was more or less predominantly black — there was some whites who lived there, but very few. There was quite a few places to play at in Kinloch, but it too has changed.[1]

I can remember one of the places there on Carson Road that was a kinda outstanding place. I think it was called the Eskimo Inn, and it was one of the largest places in Kinloch. A fellow by the name of Johnny McKnight owned the place, and I played there mostly with Roosevelt Sykes. This was in the 1930s. McKnight had different people out there, and he would employ anybody that was qualified to draw or hold a crowd together. Johnny McKnight had several brothers, and they lived down on Biddle Street. But it was mainly piano players that played there — whoever was around at the time and was respected as a musician. I think Jabo Williams also played there. He would give them all a chance. McKnight also played piano himself. I don't think he ever recorded anything himself, but locally he was just as famous as the recording stars. He was a gambler too, sort of a hustler. Some of the brothers eventually went back to Arkansas, and Johnny died. But they gambled there, and at that time gambling was a part of almost everything. The place had a pretty good reputation.

Kinloch had an East St. Louis flavor to it, and there was some pretty decent entertainment. At least you wasn't subject to too much harassment. People preferred to go to a place like that, where they wasn't gonna be pushed around all kinda ways. In the city of St. Louis, it was more pleasing to go to East St. Louis for fun than it was to stay in St. Louis. There was a lot of places in St. Louis, but you was never sure of whether you was gonna have to go to jail and stay down there. In St. Louis you might just get locked up on a Saturday night and you'd be turned loose maybe in time to go to work on Monday morning. No charges, you just locked up. It was a common thing with me when I was playing — it didn't matter with me. They used to say, "Ride down and walk back." They wouldn't bring you back, that was all there was to it.

I also saw a minstrel show once, but to tell you the truth I can't place where I saw the show at. There was a place called the Grand Theater, which was at Twentieth and Market Streets, and they used to have all these kind of things there. And at the side of the theater in the summer months they had it in the open air. The Grand was one of the two places where I saw Butterbeans and Susie. There was also Jim McMann's on Market Street. McMann's was a famous place — it was a gambling house and he had music there. But it was designed for crap games, alcohol and water, and what have you, all the unlawful stuff — a speakeasy.

Now in places like the Dance Box, which was located on Ewing, they had a cover charge and they wouldn't be held responsible if you brought your own drinks in. I guess everybody was getting something off a big show, so nobody bothered you. But they didn't actually try and sell drinks in the place. The Dance Box was a regular night club with entertainment periodically. I didn't go there too much — maybe once or twice — and I never worked there. I was too young. I was sticking my nose everywhere I could get into.[2]

But the Dance Box was a kinda classical place, and it held some of the top people. The Dance Box was a popular place but it didn't exist too long. I wouldn't be surprised if this pianist Deloise Searcy didn't play there. He was a kind of versatile guy. He played classics, blues, and what have you, and I'm reasonably sure that he played there. I remember Deloise — I can see him now — he was a kinda punkish-acting fellow. He wasn't what you would call a gut bucket blues player. He was a kind of rhythm type, updated stuff. Between blues and classics was what he was.[3]

I knew Deloise, not as buddy-buddy, but I knew him. He was an associate of another person that was also a pretty famous piano player named Robert Wrights. And he was that kind of person too, you know.[4] I don't know where Robert was from, because when I knew him he was here in St. Louis and pretty well established. I don't think he ever recorded. He was a kinda swing man — he played blues but also swing and classical styles. Robert used to entertain around St. Louis a whole lot. And he and Deloise were playing houses just like the other musicians were. Robert was a good mixer with everybody, not just his class of people. He knew how to come here where we were and be just like we are. Then when he'd get with his group he'd get just like them. He also had a wife and five kids.

I recall one time Roosevelt Sykes and I were playing over at Charley Houston's, and I remember the number we were doing, "I Got Tired of Your Low Down Dirty Ways." I was sitting down on top of the piano, an upright piano. I was sitting on the right side of Roosevelt, and I was playing my guitar, and they were out there dancin'. And some guy kept meddlin' with Robert Wrights and stepping on his feet. Robert said, "You better stay off my feet, fellow." The guy — I guess he caught himself pickin' at him. All of a sudden the guy stepped on his feet again. "I done told you to stay off my feet. You better not do that again." After a while the guy came back around, and evidently he must have tried that again. So Robert stopped dancing and went right down in his sock and pulled out a razor. He said, "I'll fix you, you so-and-so. Don't pay no attention to this sissy shit. I'm a man like you. I'll cut your fucking head off." Boy, that guy split! Oh boy, that almost broke up the party there. People just fell out laughing. But that guy moved out of there.

Deloise Searcy and Eddie Miller were what you'd call popular pianists. They were there before Roosevelt Sykes hit the scene. They played for white clubs, entertaining, and all this kinda thing. Eddie was a pretty decent piano player — he had his style and he was pretty good with it. He was versatile with it too, although you probably wouldn't hear anything on record now but a blues sound. I didn't get to meet Eddie too often. After he and his wife, Luella Miller, done their recording he was more or less visible, but Eddie was a working man and he didn't flounder around too much. Eddie had a regular job, and at one time I think he worked at a steel foundry. But he covered quite a bit of territory with his piano playing — styles, you know, classics, what have you, he wasn't just a dead blues man.

Luella and Eddie Miller lived out there near Dago Hill. You know she made that number, "Build Me a Mansion out on Dago Hill."[5] They lived over there — well, not quite. It's called Compton Hills where they lived, it's the joining of Dago Hill. It's the same hills but one of them was called Compton and a little further over it was called Dago Hill.[6] They lived quite a bit south for blacks at the time.

Now Market Street all the way over to just about LaSalle was the black belt: Market, Walnut, Eugenia, all them streets back over that way. Then there was the railroad, then it skipped over to Chouteau, LaSalle, and almost back to Park Avenue. Then there was a little pocket that went up to join the hills, and that was called Compton Hills, and some blacks were living in there. These were the blacks that had a little more than the others. Well, that's where Luella and Eddie lived.

Luella was a young woman — she was way younger than Lonnie Johnson and all of them, although she may have been slightly older than me. I don't know no place where Luella actually sang as a paying job, but I know places where she would sing. Like people be at a place and somebody would ask her to do a number, and she would sing there. I never did know her to be hired to entertain.

When Luella faded out, I think she started working for the church, something like Mary Johnson ended up doing. Luella came out of the blues and joined the church, and just a matter of time from that she passed. I couldn't name the amount of years, but it wasn't no great long time. It wasn't no eight or ten years, it was less than that, and this was from the time of her recording.

I've heard the name Al Miller mentioned time and time again, but unfortunately I never did get the chance to meet this fellow Al Miller.[7] He may have been related to them. I don't know whether Eddie played a guitar and went in and put another name on it. Also, I don't know whatever happened to Eddie Miller.

I also knew Irene Scruggs — she used to live not too far from me. They lived in the same row of flats on Nineteenth Street as Pete Bogans. The Scruggses lived next door to him. I never saw her perform and I don't really know too much about her performing. Her reputation was pretty broad, so I would assume that she had entertained quite a bit around here, but I can't recall any specific place she worked at.[8]

Jesse Johnson's record shop was at the corner of Jameson and Market Streets, but I can't visualize it being no record store there when I first started going into Funky London, which was just across the street. Jesse was at the Market Street location before he moved up onto Jefferson.[9]

Jesse Johnson was one of the first promoters out of the city of St. Louis for black artists, and he got to be known nationally from the material he sent to those companies. RCA wasn't accepting too much, and I think he broke the ice in getting them to accept black artists. He was also doing things for Okeh, Brunswick, and Paramount Records, because I was on trips with him for some of them.

I don't know who the first group of people that come through him and recorded were, but I know it wasn't too long before Roosevelt Sykes was involved. That's also where Victoria Spivey got her trip to

Okeh Records from, when she recorded "That Mean Black Snake." I don't know whether she went to New York to record or what, but Roosevelt and them went to New York.[10]

I would say Jesse Johnson was a man with influence. I don't think he was a politician, but was respected as a businessman. I don't think he had political power, but he became a renowned person and set a pretty good example for that part of the town. He proved the facts to a lot of black people that they could do a few things in the city. After he went into this record store, he then come up with a restaurant and a cab company, and that gave him a lot of publicity. People began to respect him and patronize his actions, trying to do likewise.

Sam Wolff was a Jewish fellow with a record store at 1319 Biddle Street, and he was the person responsible for me recording for Columbia Records. I was in his store periodically — you could play records, and I would go in and listen at sounds. He had those little stalls for when more than one person would come in and wanted to hear a record. You were supposed to play the record and buy it, but I would go in there and play records. He also sold musical instruments. Anyway, he heard me play guitar and he asked me to do a little thing for him.

He had one of those old crank-up disk-cutting machines. All you had to do was put a sound back into it and that needle would cut on this little disk. Not clear, but good enough to distinguish what was going on. He got three or four off of me and I guess this is what he presented to the people at Columbia Records to get their attention.

Sam Wolff was just in the sales end of the record business, but some of the people who were in the scout business from out of town knew about him, because he was one of the major sales persons in St. Louis for black music. They would ask him to do little favors for them and he'd get it together. But he wasn't like Charley Jordan or Jesse Johnson. Jesse Johnson was so popular with it because he was in the business and he had some ideas on what would and what would not be in sales, and the record companies trusted that.

Several other people had been in Wolff's store and done the same thing as me, and I guess that's where he got Sylvester Palmer involved in it. I do remember Wolff had an old piano sitting in there over against the wall. I first met Sylvester there at the store, because I didn't know anything about him before then, and at that time I'd been in St. Louis a long time. It could have been that he'd just come up from some place else out of the city.

Sylvester and I went to Chicago to record for Columbia. The studio was on Lake Shore Drive, number 666; I guess I will remember that from here on through.[11] I recorded four songs, and nobody that I know of ever uttered any of the lyrics that I sang. "Mistreating Blues" had nothing to do with other "Mistreating Blues" that you've heard, none whatsoever. It was something that had happened to me.

Sylvester Palmer had his own particular style on piano, and it was a very strange style. The one number that I think sold better was "Do It Sloopy." I haven't heard anybody come close to playing that particular style; it has a ring more towards Cow Cow Davenport than anybody that I know. And it's not really Davenport, but it has that same kind of thing.

He was a pretty nice piano player. We recorded at the same session. He had his own tunes selected and brought them to Columbia. There's spots in Sylvester's songs that fit a lot of people. Listening to his music I hear a Lonnie Johnson lick he done. I hear a lot of different piano players do what he does. I hear a little Leroy Carr in there, strange as it seems; and I hear a little Clarence Williams in there. And he had a peculiar bridge, that boom, boom.

Anyway, I didn't stay no time in Chicago — it was almost a round trip back. When the session was over, I was boarding the train coming back home. I don't remember who was in charge of the session, but a few things I do remember. I remember the address of the place and being really excited. And I remember them giving me three hundred dollars. That was a lot of money. It wasn't enough, but it was some money for what I'd done. It wasn't really a big deal, but three hundred dollars went quite a way at that time.

But we spent the three hundred dollars. I couldn't say we spent it in a tavern, because there wasn't no taverns, there were speakeasies. And I kinda relied on my elder brother's judgment on whatever was going on, and I don't know what he done with some of it. But when I reached the place where I was staying, I'd just conserved some change: twenty-five or thirty dollars.

I don't know what happened to Sylvester Palmer after the session — we kinda got split up. Sylvester was a drinker, and he didn't live too long after that recording; his health went bad. He was living here in St. Louis down on O'Fallon.[12] I think he lived long enough to hear the release of his recordings. I know my oldest brother Minnow and Sylvester had the same girlfriend for a short time, and her name was Fanny. She wasn't either one of them's wife, so it didn't make no difference — whatever she do was her business. I don't know if my brother knew that or not, but I did.

Now there's a good chance Sylvester learnt to play piano right here in St. Louis, but I'd never heard of him before. He was one of the guys like myself that was narrowly known. I didn't know any of his relatives or anything. We wasn't associates or anything before that particular session happen.

I've also heard it said that the piano player Wesley Wallace and Sylvester Palmer were one and the same person. Forget it — it's not true. At Sylvester's session I was sitting right in the studio with him, and at my session he was right in the studio with me, and there was no other person involved. And being as I'm the one fortunate enough to be alive to tell it like it happened, I'm saying exactly as it was: no Wesley Wallace. There was no other people in the studio at that session except Sylvester Palmer and Henry Townsend. We both made four songs, which meant two 78s, and that was it. And unless Sylvester made a quick return, he didn't make it back no more. Now neither did I for Columbia.

Now Wesley Wallace's sounds were toward Sylvester somewhat, but Sylvester was a Walter Davis: he didn't use the formula of music, he used his own creation. He would just make a turnaround when he got ready, whenever he felt that he should turn around within himself. Somebody working with him would be as lost as a bat. But Wesley Wallace was a little different — he had some cues at times. Sylvester never had a cue. If you notice his playing, he never cued a turn for somebody that's following him. He'd just make his bridge and go on back to the next thing. And vocally there is no similarity there.

Wesley Wallace and I was never around a whole lot together. I never played with Wesley Wallace. I heard that he lived in Alton, Illinois.

Peetie Wheatstraw was supposed to have lived in Alton too, and that's where I got this, from Peetie. That's where Peetie was supposed to have known him at.[13] Wesley Wallace had beautiful coordination with what he was doing, very timely. The introduction he plays to "Fanny Lee Blues" was a typical sound of this city, that beat. A percentage of all the piano players played that. That was one of the things that I kinda shied around. I didn't ever want that sound — I guess because everybody was doing it.

No one person that I know of could be credited with that sound — it goes all the way back. Everybody I remember from my early existence played blues sounds like that in St. Louis; that was one of the things that they could do very well. I could give no particular person credit for that basic lick.

I saw Wesley Wallace different places in St. Louis, and I think I saw him in East St. Louis a long time ago. East St. Louis is tore down so bad now I have trouble remembering, but it was somewhere down in the Third Street area, where Peetie Wheatstraw used to hang around at, down in there. Sometimes I'm on the highway and I look down in there and don't nothing look like it did then. It just don't look like that's where it was. It's difficult for me to just point out exactly where it was, but it was in that vicinity, I can say that. There's places that I've been to down on Third Street, and I couldn't go back to that spot now to save my life.[14]

✳ ✳ ✳

I knew Roosevelt Sykes before he ever recorded any records. I'm reasonably sure I met him down on Market Street at that show, Funky London. I didn't know he was a piano player when I first met him, and I can't remember who it was that made me acquainted with him. And the next time I remember seeing him was at Jesse Johnson's music shop. I also ran into Roosevelt over on Compton, somewhere over that way in south St. Louis. He was living on the street south of LaSalle at the time and he was playing some little places over that way. I really don't think he was playing for money — I think it was just because he could play the piano. He would go to places where people had a piano in the house and he'd play. This was in the 1920s.

I knew Roosevelt before I met Walter Davis. Roosevelt and I was bummin' around quite a bit then. Roosevelt played just about all them clubs in St. Louis. He played at Jazzland, which was pretty close to DeLuxe Music on Market Street, on the same side of the street.

I would play with Sykes occasionally, but a lot of times I wouldn't even have a guitar with me, I'd just go and visit where he played, something like that. In later years I started carrying my axe everywhere I went. The reason I started playing with Roosevelt was his baby brother, Walter. Walter and I were together pretty diligent all over, even though I knew Roosevelt before any of his brothers.

Walter Sykes was as good or better than Roosevelt on piano. He couldn't sing as strong and as good as Roosevelt, but his execution was beautiful. But Walter would travel so much until I didn't want to do the extreme amount of traveling that he done. He was also a kind of a pimp too, and he had a couple of gals that seeked his well-being, and it wasn't quite my game, you know what I mean. He and I associated quite a bit, but he would go out of town with no job, just go, and I wasn't for traveling like that. And he would take his women with him — that was his source.

Now there was another brother that come here from Helena, Arkansas, and his name was Jesse. He also played piano. He wasn't as good as Roosevelt and Walter, but I started banging around with Jesse. I'd take him over on Delmar, 21 something on Delmar. This lady had a kind of a good time house, and we'd play there. Roosevelt would come by once in a while when we'd be there, and he'd just hear us playing. And when Walter had made his rounds and got back, he and I would get together. Well, Roosevelt got a little jealous. He had more to offer me than Walter and Jesse, so he said, "Come on and go with me." So that's when I started playing with Roosevelt.

Roosevelt was here in St. Louis before any of his brothers. Walter only lived here periodically — he'd come in and out, in and out. Jesse, when he did come, he stayed. And Willie was a kid; he wasn't a Sykes and he never did leave the south. Willie played too, but he was just like a beginner — he never did get too good. But now he also had another half-brother named Johnny, and he was real good. Johnny Sykes was the oldest. They all grew up with an organ in the home, and

Roosevelt told me that he used to play in church on organ, play sacred stuff on the organ.

Jesse Johnson was the guy that promoted Roosevelt to Victor and record companies from different places. When I started working with Roosevelt we'd run on the same trips through Jesse Johnson. When Roosevelt first recorded for Okeh Records, Jesse took them to the studio in New York. I didn't get in on that session at all; I wanted to, but I didn't make it. Roosevelt's first record was the "44 Blues." Clifford Gibson went with him that time.

Clifford and Roosevelt were together quite a bit at that particular time. And I'm pretty sure Clifford was on guitar with him on "All My Money's Gone." And I think he's on "The Way I Feel" and "Henry Ford"; I think he worked with him entirely on that session. "Tired of Being Mistreated" is definitely Clifford Gibson. I think that's the same session I'm talking about.[15]

Lee Green was the originator of the "44 Blues" and Roosevelt and Little Brother Montgomery and so on. Little Brother claims he taught it to Lee Green, but he must have taught an awful old man some music, and him being pretty young. Lee Green was way older than Little Brother Montgomery. All of them was up in a bracket, but Lee Green was older, in my opinion. I never did ask his age, but you get an idea from seeing the people and what they do in life. Lee Green had Roosevelt, I guess, as much as five years. That "44 Blues," there's no telling where that thing came from. Little Brother Montgomery called it "Vicksburg Blues." But Roosevelt brought it to the fame under the title "44 Blues."

It's like the "Cairo Blues": who knows where that particular sound come from, it goes way back before my time. It goes way back before Henry Spaulding's time. There's no telling where it come from, could've been fifty years before then, who knows? Somebody got it from somebody and so on. I know I hear lyrics that my daddy used to sing when I was a little boy and they come forth after I got to be a man to go on records, so who knows?

Lee Green really played the "44 Blues," but it was a different style from Roosevelt's though. He had his own style. The truth is, personally I liked his style better than I did Roosevelt's, his little funny riffs and things — it amused me. The similarities were there, but Roosevelt's was a little more bold than his, and I liked the little unbold.

I'm sure I heard from Roosevelt that Lee Green is kind of responsible for a few of the things that he played on piano. Lee Green kind of put Roosevelt under his arm in a sense, kind of father him out in a lot of places. He kind of see to Roosevelt direction-wise, going in the right direction and doing the right things in the music field too. They were really good buddies, I know that.

Lee Green would come into St. Louis and stay a length of time and then leave, but he lived here quite a spell. He lived on Seventeenth Street, and I think he's the cause of Roosevelt moving on Seventeenth Street. It was a kind of a speakeasy place on Seventeenth between Wash and Franklin. Lee would do his own entertaining there and sell his own alcohol and water. If he was playing and he wanted some juice, he'd get up and get it and go back to playing. He also played at Charley Houston's place, and I think he played at the Royal Candy Kitchen on Market Street. Roosevelt also played there a long time. It was a candy shop up the front but they had other activities going on. It was a pretty neat place — it was about the neatest place down there after the Booker Washington thing had gone down. It was right across the street from the Booker Washington near Jefferson.

When I first started going over to East St. Louis to amount to anything, it must have been the top of the twenties, because that's when I first met Walter Davis. Walter had just come to East St. Louis, and he was doing a little cleaning up for a guy named J. C. who owned a club there right next to a switch railroad line that ran into a junkyard on Fifteenth Street. It's near the place where the city of East St. Louis store all their trucks and equipment. Anyway, on the switch line they'd sit boxcars to be loaded with metal and iron, and sometimes they would sit there a week before they'd get to it, and that's where Walter was staying. He was sleeping out there and I guess kind of earning his food. Roosevelt played there periodically, and Walter wanted to participate; he felt like he could sing, and Roosevelt gave him a try. If Roosevelt would be working and get tired, he'd shift somebody in there to help him out.

So that's where Walter got his start. Roosevelt was instrumental in getting him started, and he finally brought Walter over to St. Louis with him. Walter wasn't playing piano then, none whatever. He didn't know one key from another. All he knew was there was black on some of the keys and white on the others — that's all he knew. Walter was around Roosevelt with the piano, but the truth is, I am the one who started Walter on the piano. I give him more information on it, teaching him. Most people ask me when did Walter Davis teach me piano, or I play just like Walter Davis, but they got it backwards. I can understand why it's so hard for them to understand. We do play the same keys, but he used a different format from me. He crosses the tonic and I stay direct in the tonic. Walter used G, B, and D — that's his chords for G, G is the tonic. I use G, D, and B in another form, same key but mine is up. His D is lower than the G. He also added a C to his.

Roosevelt was very instrumental in getting me started with the piano. I can say he's totally the reason I went into it as much as I did. We had a trade deal there — he never did get to be as good with the guitar as I have with the piano, but he did play guitar. He got me off into the piano way back — it had to be in the 1920s because in the 1930s I done a recording, "All I've Got's Gone" on piano.[16]

Walter didn't play piano on his first records. When he played anything on his records I was backing him up on guitar. Sykes played for him in the beginning on up for quite a spell, until him and Sykes kinda fell out. He was trying to learn to play the piano then, and I supported him in teaching him a lot of piano licks and backing him with the guitar. I showed him sounds to put on the piano to correspond with his vocals and all that. I was very instrumental with him doing these kind of things, very helpful to him. And of course he had his own ideas when he got started into it.

Roosevelt was living on Seventeenth Street with his wife Leola, and that's where I first met Charlie McFadden at, down there on Seventeenth Street. We called him Specks, and I met him through Roosevelt Sykes. I don't know where Charlie was from; I heard rumors that he was from somewhere in Tennessee, but this come from somebody that I don't put too much stock in, so I don't know where Charlie was from. We didn't do too much work as a group, the three of us. I was either with Roosevelt or with Charlie or Walter Davis. I would go around sometimes with Roosevelt and Charlie, but I never would insert any sounds in what they would be doing because it would always be a job for Roosevelt. Charlie, Roosevelt, and I were all kind of buddy-buddies, and we'd be together two or three times a week at least.

Charlie was a real nice guy. He'd had some kind of accident and he lost one of his eyes. As it was told to me — and I think it was true because Roosevelt was the one that told me — some gal that he was living with put his eye out in some kind of skirmish, a fight or something. It was done purposely, it wasn't no accident. I know he wasn't married to nobody. He had that eye covered all the time — he wore that patch. He also had great big thick glasses — you know the kind, where you look at them and the eyes look bigger — great big thick rims that looked like some of those jelly glasses with gold metal frames.

"Piggly Wiggly" was Charlie's number, "Groceries on the Shelf." Piggly Wiggly were the first help yourself markets. Piggly Wiggly had come up into Cairo, and that was the only one that I knew about. There were others in Chicago in later years, but I'm talking about in the beginning — that's the Piggly Wiggly that I know about. That song done fairly well. He'd be around with Roosevelt quite a bit and he'd just do vocals. Occasionally he and I would get together, and if I backed him up he would play piano, but not without a backup — he wouldn't challenge it by himself.[17]

Charlie was also taught to play by Roosevelt. Roosevelt would help him out, but Charlie had his own little thing that he would do. He had a little tune — I got a little of it, but I never did get it all. It was a little tune he played in A-flat, and I've never heard anyone play it but him. Roosevelt used to come close towards it after he heard Charlie doing it, but he could never get it like Charlie had it. He had a peculiar little sound.

Charlie McFadden had money when nobody else had money. Charlie would walk about with two or three hundred dollars in his pocket when people were hungry. His money was in a tobacco sack, one of them old Bull Durham tobacco sacks. When they found Charlie at his death, I think he was worth a few grand. He was staying in an old building, taking care of the place — it was on Twenty-second or Twenty-third Street, somewhere over in there — where they found him. It wasn't a house at all; it had been some kind of enterprise, and he had little quarters that he had put in there. I guess the owner put him in there because he would kinda protect the place. It may have been a job for him, but the building wasn't being used for nothing.

I know one time I went by there and he was talking about what he should do; he didn't believe in fooling with no banks. And he counted about twenty-nine or thirty one hundred dollar bills plus some twenties. I don't know how many twenties he had, but when he was counting the hundred dollar bills I was there. He maybe had a stack an inch high of twenties. And it wasn't too long after he was found dead in there.

He died of natural causes, no foul play. I don't know too much on that, but I feel it would have been sometime in the early 1940s, sometime before I went to the army. It had to be, because I didn't see him after I come out of service. I can stay with the forties because Roosevelt was in Chicago and I talked with him about did I see Charlie. That was before I went in the army. Of course I wasn't in the army very long, but when I come out I didn't see him anymore. This is the time I heard about him. I must have saw Charlie for the last time about June or July of 1944, just before I went into the army.[18]

Miss Callie's was on Twenty-first and Delmar — her and her husband Henry had a house there, 2112 Delmar — and this is where Jesse Sykes and I used to get together and play a whole lot. This is also where I organized a club so that things would be, on the surface anyway, on the up and up. We got our papers and all the stuff from downtown to put our license on the wall. And if and when the police come to raise hell, the first thing they would face would be this license. That would cool their ambitions down a little bit because it was legalized. But if they went further, well, it was a different thing.

It worked out good — matter of fact there was never a raid there. But the same things went on there. It was a survival act really, and quite a few homes had found ways to survive, and there wasn't too much trouble if you knew how to go about getting that camouflage. There was a lot of clubs and social clubs organized during this time. Anyway, this is where I met J. D. Short at; he was rooming at Miss Callie's place.

When J. D. first come to St. Louis he was playing a teenie bit of guitar, but not to be listened at. He had a little something that he could do. I think his inspiration came out of the South, and that's where all his sounds were embedded from — whatever he done, he developed it from that. He had an act when he sang where he could tremble his jaw some kind of way, and they called him Jelly Jaw. We never did actually play together.[19]

One time I was hired to play at a house on Twenty-second and Wash, somewhere in there. I had the weekends and J. D. Short had some other time, I don't know exactly what it was. So this is where he and I was, and I don't know today what caused the problem, but it was on one of the weekends when I was playing there.

I had done a little short session, and J. D. and I hadn't said anything but hi to one another. I was standing up talking to somebody and he said to me, "Look out, Henry!" I threw my arm up and caught that blade right in the back. Anyway, I wheeled around and I knocked J. D. down behind that, then I started for the back door. Some people had also started to run and they blocked me, and he got a chance to stick me again right in the back. I was running from it because I didn't have no knife, and I knew I couldn't stand up with bare hands to no knife blade.

Anyway, I got out of the place and into the gangway, and he came out of the door and into the gangway. But I had stumbled on a big brick, so I got that and hit it up against the wall and broke it in two. Now he was coming down the aisle and I can't miss him because it's a little narrow gangway, just the size of a person plus a little bit.

I turned that brick loose and knocked him down again, but he got up and started at me again. I was just about at the street when I let the other half of that brick a loose and I knocked him down again. This time he turned and run back and jumped the fence. I walked across the street and that was as far as I could get. I'd bled so through this back wound I was too weak to go any further.

The blade went in deep — it touched my lungs. So I sat down and an undertaker come across the street! The live man walking over to the undertaker! But somebody got hold to the policeman and they got me to City Hospital Number Two, which at that time was over on

Lawton. At that time those doctors there were well known. If you go there cut or injured, your head cut, don't worry about it because you'll live, they'll put you back together. But if you go there with a headache, that will be it because they don't know nothing about that! Them old black doctors over there really knew how to handle bruised-up people. They put me back together, and it was serious — I was in hospital about a week.

The first time I saw J. D. Short after that was across town at a gambling joint called T. J.'s. This could be confused with J. C.'s, but this was T. J.'s. I had been told that he was there, so I went there looking for him. Anyway, he spotted me a little bit before I spotted him.

I saw him when he got up and went into the bathroom. When I made it back to the bathroom, wasn't anybody in there — he got out of a little window. Looked like to me the window was too little for him to get out of. I really didn't know what I was going to do, but I knew the score wasn't settled. I had a pistol with me, so it could have well be said that my intention was to kill him. And it was a long time before I saw him again. I heard about him being somewhere else, but whoever told me must have went back and told him, because when I got there he wasn't there.

The next time I saw him was on Tenth Street, and nobody told me nothing. The police station was on Tenth and Carr, and there was an alley behind the police station that went over to Biddle Street. There were houses in that alley, and he was sitting over there playing. I heard the playing and I went through the gangway and peeped through there and I knew it was him. He didn't see me this time. I came out of the alleyway at Tenth and Biddle and went all the way to Eleventh and Division — that's where John M. lived. Now I knew John M. had a .38, and I knew he kept it in the kitchen up where the alcohol and water was.

John M. was in the front room. He didn't worry about me — he knows I ain't gonna do nothing wrong. But this time I did. I went in there and got me a half-pint and stuck it in my pocket and got that .38. I checked it, and it was loaded all the way 'round. I walked out there and said, "John, I'll be back in a few minutes." And I hit the street.

I ran all the way back there. I walked on through the gangway, and he looked up and saw me. He jumped straight up and ran his hand in his pocket for that knife again. I said, "Oh no, it won't work this time." But he started towards me. I said, "Stop." I think what I wanted to know more than anything else was why. Because today I still don't know why. But he wouldn't stop walking towards me with that knife. I asked him three times, I said, "Don't come no further."

Now he ain't seen no gun and I guess he figured, well, so what? The next time I asked him, and he made that next step. Pow! I hit him. I wasn't shooting at no particular place, I was shooting at him. But you know what? I knocked it off — I castrated him, the first shot, and I didn't shoot no more. When I hit him, he jumped straight up in the air and fell down and went to quivering. I turned around and went on back and put John M.'s pistol up and hit the road. I didn't know if I'd killed him or not.

I went to East St. Louis and grabbed me a freight train. I went to Cairo, Illinois, and I went down to Memphis for a while and I just floated around. I wouldn't stay put too long, and I was gone for about four months. I stayed away until I felt things were all right, and then I come back.

But nothing ever developed out of it — nobody ever came to my folks' house looking for me. How I know what happened to him was through Neckbones and Tobe Williams. They were the ones that knew what happened. They had to remove his bollocks, his whole nut bag — so I called it even, then. But I'm pretty sure I've figured out the reason for his actions — or as close as I can without ever really being able to know. I figure that the man was absolutely jealous of me and my music. I didn't see it necessary for him to feel that way, because he had his thing and was respected very much for what he done.

But after that last episode, I wasn't concerned no more. I kinda felt like I'm even. I don't know what made me feel that way, but I had my revenge. Maybe if I'd shot him in the arm I might not have felt as well as I felt when I cut his balls out. You know it's just something in a person — it could have been the very evil in me — but revenge is sweet, I can tell you that.

If J. D. had really knew me, when he cut me he shouldn't have let me live. I guess he didn't intend to let me live, but he didn't know me as well as he thought he did. When he cut me he ought to have left town, tried to hide for keeps. If he had known me, he would have known that I was gonna find him sooner or later. I left home originally because I didn't want no whoopin'. He should have thought, "Now I done whipped a man that when he was a boy wouldn't stand a whoopin'. Now he's a man and I've done something to him." Now he'd have fled away from that.

But you know what? Down through the years we met, but I was very alert; I suppose he was too, but he never mentioned it, and neither did I. This is true. The last time I saw J. D. was on Twenty-fifth and Franklin, and he told me where he lived. But you know, I wouldn't be no fool. I would not have went to his house if it wasn't but one house in the world!

Twentieth and O'Fallon Streets, St. Louis, circa 1920s.
(Courtesy of Swekosky Collection)

"Henry's Worry Blues" was recorded during Henry Townsend's first session for Columbia in 1929. (Photograph by Bill Greensmith)

"Long Ago Blues" was recorded during Henry Townsend's first session for Columbia in 1929. (Photograph by Bill Greensmith)

This is the only known copy of Henry Townsend's "Jack of Diamonds Georgia Rub" from 1930. (Photograph by Doug Seroff)

Joe Dean, St. Louis, circa 1930.
*(Courtesy of Mike Rowe/*Blues Unlimited*)*

Charley Jordan,
circa 1930.
(Courtesy of
Paul Garon)

Lonnie Johnson on
guitar with an unknown
bass player in Chicago in
1941. (Courtesy of FSA
Collection)

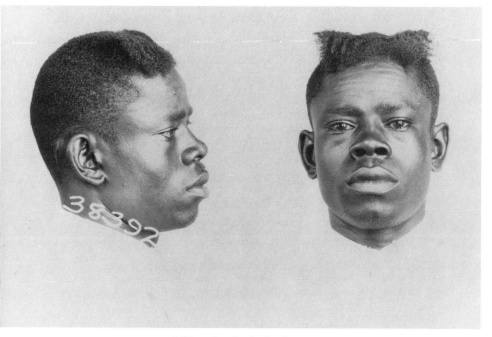

Milton Sparks, St. Louis, 1934.
*(Courtesy of Mike Rowe/*Blues Unlimited*)*

Robert Nighthawk, circa early 1940s.
(Courtesy of Blues Unlimited*)*

opposite: Allen Townsend, St. Louis, circa 1940s. (Henry Townsend's collection)

Front row, left to right: *Muddy Waters, John Lee "Sonny Boy" Williamson, Lacy Belle, unknown man.* Back row, left to right: *Unknown boy, Eddie Boyd, unknown woman. Chicago, mid-1940s. (Courtesy of* Blues Unlimited*)*

opposite: Henry Townsend, St. Louis, circa mid-1940s.
(Henry Townsend's collection)

Walter Davis,
St. Louis, late 1940s.
(Photograph by Willie Feagan;
Bill Greensmith's collection)

Eleventh and Biddle Streets, St. Louis, late 1940s.
(Courtesy of Swekosky Collection)

The 1700 block of Market Street, St. Louis, late 1940s.
(Courtesy of Swekosky Collection)

Grand Central Hotel, St, Louis, late 1940s.
(Courtesy of Swekosky Collection)

Walter Davis, "Tears Came Rollin' Down," 1952. (Photograph by Bill Greensmith)

Tommy Bankhead and Henry Townsend, Technisonic Studios, St. Louis, 17 May 1961. (Photograph by Charley O'Brien)

Barrelhouse Buck, Alton, Illinois, 1961.
(Photograph by Charley O'Brien)

Big Joe Williams,
England, 1963.
(Courtesy of
Blues Unlimited*)*

Henry Townsend and Roosevelt Sykes, circa 1970. (Henry Townsend's collection)

Sunnyland Slim and Henry Townsend, St. Louis, 1981.
(Henry Townsend's collection)

Henry Townsend, St. Louis, 1984.
(Photograph by Bill Greensmith)

Vernell and Henry Townsend,
Chicago Blues Festival, June 1986.
(Photograph by Bill Greensmith)

opposite: Henry Townsend, St. Louis, 1986. (Photograph by Bill Greensmith)

Henry Townsend, St. Louis, 1987.
(Photograph by Bill Greensmith)

Robert Jr. Lockwood and Henry Townsend, St. Louis, 1988.
(Photograph by Bill Greensmith)

Henry
Townsend
and Yank
Rachell, St.
Louis, 1989.
(Photograph
by Bill
Greensmith)

Henry Townsend's star on the St. Louis Walk of Fame, Delmar Avenue.
(Photograph by Bill Greensmith)

four

"HAVE FUN WITH IT"

I remember distinctly going up to Wisconsin one time to record for Paramount Records. It was a chair factory where the studio was located. I guess the location was suitable for them, and they just moved things around and set the studio up. It wasn't actually a studio; they set a studio up in it because it had good acoustics. I didn't know too much about acoustics then — don't know too much about that part of it now — but I do understand that the sound wasn't like a reverb, wouldn't come back in on you. And I think they finally made a studio in this place where they manufactured chairs. It was right around the lake from Chicago.[1]

I don't remember any of the people who were handling things at Paramount by name, but Jesse Johnson was involved in that setup. I don't know of anybody else from St. Louis that would've had anything to do with that at the time. Anyone who was up there recording at that time from this part of the country was with Jesse Johnson. On that session was Roosevelt Sykes, Charlie McFadden, and this boy, Oliver Cobb.

Jesse Johnson was a unique guy. He was a reasonable type, average type of fellow, but strictly business. Nice personality but not necessarily an easy-going guy. He wasn't one of them cantankerous people; if you stayed straight with him, he stayed straight with you. Of course he was shrewd, very shrewd. Sometimes he'd be driving the car and we'd get as far as Bloomington or somewhere like that and we'd be ready for some food. He stuttered, and he'd say, "You guys go in here and eat dinner, but eat like you eat at home. Don't go in there and order no beef solid, get your beef ground up, get you a hamburger. This is coming out of my pocket."

Now "Doctor, Oh Doctor," I remember that title, but "Jack of Diamonds Georgia Rub," I didn't remember it. I'm not saying I didn't do it, because I didn't remember "Candy Man" until heard it again.[2] They've got all my material everywhere else.[3] Both "Doctor, Oh Doctor" and "Candy Man" had gone from my memory for keeps until it was brought back to me. I was asked about "Candy Man" and I couldn't find nothing in my mind about it until I heard it, then it dawned on me exactly.[4]

Oliver Cobb worked around St. Louis quite a bit — he was a pretty famous guy around here. I could say without too much doubt that he worked with Jeeter-Pillars's band and this guy that's got the undertaker's, Eddie Randle.[5] Oliver Cobb was more jazz than blues. He could play blues, but seemingly his desire was to be in the jazz field. But even at that time he got more calls for blues styles. That's why he got a chance to go up on the session, because he kind of put himself into the category of playing the blues, and that's what was in demand. Because if he'd been living with his jazz, he'd never got a chance to go along with us.

People like Oliver Cobb and Jeeter-Pillars, they had almost permanent jobs. Sometimes Oliver had his own thing together and other times he was a sideman with a number of people. He was a great imitation of Louis Armstrong, great towards Armstrong. The closest I've heard — and I've heard a lot since his time doing Louis's stuff — but Oliver was right in Louis's tracks with his sounds.

When Oliver Cobb came back from Wisconsin, he stopped in Chicago and somehow he got drowned. It wasn't foul play or anything. They say he got to whiskey drinking, and you know drinking and water gives you problems. At that time they used to have a stretch across out there in the lake that you could go beyond if you want to, but you were at your own risk. A lot of guys used to think that this was a sport thing to do, to show that they didn't have to play it safe. And he had a few drinks and felt that he could show off, and he went beyond the line and they couldn't get to him in time. This was in Lake Michigan.

Oliver was playing up until the time he went to record for Paramount. Whatever weekend it was before we went to Wisconsin, he was probably engaged. We went there and recorded and it wasn't no solid week before he drowned. As close as that. You can bet it wasn't no more than a week to the recording from the last engagement he had. I know after that particular time Cobb didn't record anymore because he couldn't record from the grave.[6]

Edith Johnson was also with us at Paramount that particular time, but I don't recall her recording anything at that time or playing piano on Oliver Cobb's recording.[7] If Edith could play piano, then I have no knowledge of it, and I'm sure I would have known something about it. I was at rehearsals time and time again with Edith, and I never saw her sit down on a piano stool to make any effort to direct the thing that she was gonna do. She just stayed aside for the vocals and Roosevelt done the playing, to my knowledge, all the way. I'm reasonably sure Oliver Cobb was also backed up by Roosevelt, because he didn't have a piano player with him.

Edith Johnson was Jesse's wife and it turned out to be his sister-in-law, as his brother Harry remarried her. I guess they didn't have no children — I think the biblical statement says there's nothing wrong with it. I wouldn't want it, but that's what it says, unless the blood has mixed. And if the blood hasn't mixed, well forget it, go ahead on with it.

Now some things are real faint to me, but it seems like I was in the studio with Red Mike at some time or another, but I can't pinpoint it.[8] Red Mike was one of the best comedians, in my opinion, that ever lived. Redd Foxx was good, but he couldn't touch Red Mike. Red Mike could take anything you say and turn it into comedy. You would have to laugh at that fellow just as long as he wanted you to laugh. Mike Bailey was his name, and he was real, real dark skinned, and he called himself Red. That was one of his comic things right there.

To my knowledge Red Mike had no job anywhere. He would do his little type of hustling. This was more or less the depression time when I knew a lot about him, so there probably wasn't no jobs for him to work. I guess he was in the category with all the rest of us — didn't necessary suffer too bad, but he didn't have all he needed. He had enough to get by with. I didn't actually see him barefooted like I saw a lot of people with no shoes.

Red Mike used to hang around Sykes all the time, when Roosevelt was living there in the alley in the 1600 block between Carr and Cole. They had a little thing going on in there. Roosevelt also used to be in the alcohol business. Walter Davis lived about two houses away directly behind where Roosevelt lived. Walter was living with a lady named Mary — this was right after he made his first recording, that "M and O" thing.[9] Red Mike used to be there at Roosevelt's house quite a bit. He'd come there and practice his songs and what have you.

He went into the recording because he could do some nice vocals and he used a little bit of his gift in the comedy field with his vocals. But I often wondered why he didn't go into the comedy part, because he was sure enough great. I don't know what ever happened to Red Mike — he disappeared. But I think in later years he joined the Greater Union Missionary Baptist Church.

Jesse Johnson organized my session for Victor Records.[10] Jesse was more or less a general scout for all the companies. If he got some talent together for one company and they didn't accept it, he'd just take them on to another one. And the success he'd had getting in talent — the companies wasn't afraid to take a chance because Roosevelt, Walter Davis, and Edith Johnson didn't do too bad.

His brother Stump didn't do too bad, and many more that I probably don't know anything about. I'm not sure, but there is a good possibility that he was involved with Lonnie Johnson. When Lonnie was in St. Louis, Jesse, to my knowledge, was the only somebody who had authority to go in for this kind of thing. He probably had something to do with that. I know Luella Miller came through him.

It would give him prestige with the record companies. These people made good hits, sold real good. So if Jesse said, "I want to bring you something," I know they would say, "All right." And he did that with a lot of us. I never did go, but he carried people for Brunswick Records. He handled Roosevelt as long as he was in the city of St. Louis. He could have been involved with Henry Spaulding, some of the people that I wasn't up tight with and saw daily. Jesse could have picked them, take them, and bring them back before I knew anything about it.

Anyway, Roosevelt, Walter Davis, Clifford Gibson, my brother Minnow, and myself recorded for Victor Records. My brother never did do any professional singing, and this was his first time trying for a recording. He had done a lot of rehearsing with us in private and occasionally he would get out. Whenever he would get around Roosevelt or myself, he would try to sing, but I never knew him to make no attempt with anybody else. He never was considered a professional by himself or anybody else. But there were a handful of people who would admire him when he sing.

I'm reasonably sure I played guitar on Minnow's record and Roosevelt played piano for him. My brother cut "Dresser Drawers."[11] I think the lyrics in the song were, "I bought my baby a dresser for Christmas, / and she lets me ramble all in her drawers." That's the way it goes. Christmas took the sting out of it, just left the suggestion there. I know some of the lyrics to "Pistol Shy," but I never heard it played back. And I never heard "Staggering Blues" — I don't know if it was ever released or not.

I know some records don't say nothing about Roosevelt — they say Willie Kelly or something — I know I'm on one of them. Roosevelt come up with Willie Kelly, Dobby Bragg, he had a whole lot of names. Then again, there could be other things that I was there for. I done a lot of being there, and don't recall being there.

I accompanied Sykes on "As Kind as I've Been to You," the song that says, "now lookie here baby, / is that the way you intend to do, / mistreating me for someone else, / as kind as I've been to you." I remember backing him up on that one, and I remember feeling kinda delighted about that song.[12]

Now "Hard Luck Man," I'm reasonably sure Clifford Gibson was playing guitar with him on that one.[13] I didn't do a whole lot of recording with Roosevelt. As close as I can come to it would be no more than two cuts. "Sunshine Special" may have been the other number that I played on with Roosevelt. At that time he was doing several numbers out in the entertaining field of that type.[14] Like "Sunnyland," "Sunshine Special," and another song he used to play — I don't think he ever recorded it — something about the Illinois Central Railroad. He was doing them kind of numbers. "Sunshine Special" probably was one that I worked with him on. It wasn't more than two numbers, I'm sure of that.

Clifford Gibson and me buddy-buddied around town quite a bit. Clifford was in on a lot of these things that I'm talking about. The Ville was his hangout; when you get to the Ville, you'd find Clifford sooner or later. Clifford was never a downtown guy; he supported the feeling that he was an aristocrat, so he kinda stayed put according to his beliefs. He'd come downtown, but it wasn't his bag.[15]

The type of work Clifford done was almost always private duties for families. Maybe a chauffeur or whatever happens in that category of job. He was a cook — he done a lot of stuff like that. If it was a hotel, he'd do butler work. He was a guy that felt that if he shouldn't be at a certain place, then he wouldn't be there, pridewise.

He didn't play a whole lot house parties, but it wasn't because he wouldn't play at them. But like I said, we were on different ends of town and there wasn't a whole lot of great transportation then. Somehow or another the average musician didn't jump the streetcar too much. So that made it a little less getting together.

Clifford didn't have no person he didn't want to work with — anybody would do Gibson because he knew what he could do. He wasn't shy of somebody that would do more than he'd do, that he would be looked down on. He wasn't shy of that and neither was I. We'd get together and just go out there and have fun with it. But now there was a lot of others that didn't feel that way. J. D. Short, I'm assuming he didn't feel that way. I could probably think of more of them that didn't think that way. Peetie Wheatstraw didn't quite feel that way — he really didn't prefer to work with no guitar players.

If Roosevelt Sykes ever run across somebody that he thought had a good enough voice and qualified, it would give him a chance to do another recording session; it was a personal interest thing. He'd get them over there and he'd get a chance to make him some money. They sang and he played for them. He carried a lot of people over to record.

Georgia Boyd was one who recorded. She was a singer but she wasn't a popular person around town. She was Johnny McKnight's girlfriend; she was his major woman.[16] Another singer was Dorothea Trowbridge, and she was Roosevelt's girlfriend at one time, so I'm reasonably sure this was how she managed to get on record. I think Roosevelt or Jesse Johnson kinda maneuvered it. She was singing fairly regularly, but with no particular person, just any place. She done quite a bit of entertaining around town in the early 1930s. Dorothea was reasonably good — she was about like Edith Johnson, I would put her in that class. And I'm not too sure whether Edith wasn't Dorothea's idol, as she would kinda sound like her in certain cases.[17]

Isabel Sykes was Roosevelt's wife at this time. She was a good vocalist and she used to follow Roosevelt around. She was to Roosevelt what my wife Vernell was to me. She would just sing with him on jobs — she never was included in the job. That's why she made the record, because she was Roosevelt's wife. He married her when her daughter Marion was three or four years old. He wasn't married to her no long extensive time — that didn't hold on. The marriage probably collapsed shortly after they recorded together.[18]

I remember those recording sessions, but when you've been on session after session they get scrambled on you, and it's not a couple of days ago when this took place. It was way back when my mama was a little girl. I think Roosevelt was involved with the session where I cut "My Sweet Candy." Edith Johnson was at the session and Napoleon Fletcher was too.[19] I think Napoleon Fletcher's gone now, but a few years back I saw him in the neighborhood down around Garrison where he was living. He was out there singing pretty well during the time Joe Dean and all them was out there. He wasn't a full-time singer, he was just one of the guys that happened in and could sing. He had somebody else play piano for him one time named Knapps or something.[20]

Now I think Roosevelt played with Carl Rafferty at one time. I've forgotten the name of this piano player that was with Carl, but they were two pretty close buddies. Carl made a record of "Dresser with the Drawers," but that was a mix-up — that title belonged to my brother.[21] Of course Roosevelt made the number again since himself. I think Roosevelt gave my brother that song, that "Dresser Drawers" thing. I also saw Carl not too long ago, maybe four or five years ago, but I've heard he's passed since then.

St. Louis had a lot of people recording at sometime or another. There was a gal here, she was not the original, but she was a Bessie Smith number two. She was a vocalist, but I don't know of any places she worked. But she was worrisome — St. Louis Bessie Smith would haunt you to death. I can see her now — boy, she was a worrisome gal. She sure enough wanted to do some recording. She was really enthused over that thing — that was her night and day talking. And so was Dorothea. They were two people that eat and slept the damn thing. Bessie Smith and Dorothea would really bother me and Sykes quite often. But Sykes didn't play for Dorothea, I'm pretty sure. Bessie tried to get me to work with her from time to time, but I never did. Maybe Henry Brown worked with her, I don't know. But I know she called for me a couple of times, and I didn't go. I didn't see no benefit to me. The truth was, there wasn't nothing in it for her either but the trip, and I didn't care about that because I'd go where I want anyway.[22]

I remember Alice Moore. She was a beautiful person, a kind-hearted person. She was a very nice-looking black gal. She was almost what you would call a pretty girl. She had a beautiful smooth skin like velvet. I think that had a lot to do with her death too. It sounds kinda off the wall, but sometimes a lot of things are against a person that don't have an understanding about how to handle it. I think it con-tributed to her living a little fast.

Alice Moore, Ike Rogers, and Henry Brown was a trio. I never worked with them, but I was around them quite a bit. All of that started at Charley Houston's; matter of fact, Alice roomed there at Charley Houston's place. Alice seemed to be slightly my senior, but not by no big difference. But from maturity, she seemed to be a little more mature than I was.

Her "Black and Evil" was a hit right away, that first one.[23] She was a pretty black woman — ain't no doubt about that — but the evil part, she wasn't evil, I don't think. But I never was her man, and that's the only way you're ever going to find that out. She may have been, but she never did show it on the surface; she always showed kindness, everybody like her.

I don't know how Alice died or why. It appears to me like I would have heard about it or somebody would have said something about it, as many people that knew her and me. I'm inclined to believe that whenever she died, it was one of the times that I was away for some reason. A lot of the stuff Alice recorded Henry Brown worked with her, but Jimmy Gordon played piano on one of her sessions. I met Jimmy in Chicago; he was pretty famous around there for a long time, but I don't remember Jimmy ever playing in St. Louis.

I used to play with a guy name Johnny Hawkins. He played piano, and his favorite style of music was this up-tempo boogie style, and he was really good on piano too. He never did no recording or nothing — he was a local musician. We worked out in the neighborhood around Ninth Street and a couple of places there on Biddle Street. But most of our playing was at his home because he was always entertaining on account of the business he had — his alcohol business — and that would help draw his crowd.

Johnny Hawkins was an extra good piano player. He was somewhat older than me, and he also had a brother named S. Q. Hawkins, who was about my age, and he also played piano. S. Q. might have played piano for somebody on some recording, I'm not sure, but he wasn't as good as his brother. Johnny died of some kind of respiratory condition sometime in the 1950s.

The last time I saw Joe Dean was at a drugstore there on Grand Avenue and North Market. Joe Dean was a real peculiar guy. He wasn't such a steady guy when he was doing his piano work; he'd get drunk, fall down, and hurt himself. If he didn't do that, he'd bother the wrong people and they'd beat him up. He just had one hell of a time. It was very rare you'd see him without a bruise or scar on his face. He more or less stayed drunk — he was heavy into it. The first thing you'd know, he'd be out on the sidewalk, where he'd just go down. And in those days you wouldn't actually get killed, but people would take advantage of you. That always has been. They'd take his money and his shoes, if he had decent shoes. He liked to dress pretty well, but each time he left home, if he had on a good suit it would be messed up by the time he'd get back home. He just couldn't handle that whiskey. He used to do a lot of work around town when they could catch him sober enough. He would go there sober, but before the thing was over, he'd be drunk.

There was a guy that used to work with Joe Dean, and his name was Joe Harding. He played guitar and he was a friend of mine. Joe Dean used to tell him, "Look, don't you do like I do. You'll be going wrong if you do. I know I'm wrong and I don't care. I don't want you doing that." But as far as music was concerned, Joe Dean was really in the bracket, in the upper bracket. If he had not come out of it, he'd have been dead way before he was, because nobody could stay that drunk and keep on living no longevity.[24]

I also played some with Barrelhouse Buck — he was my old buddy. Buck was senior to me somewhat. His name was McFarland, and he was a pretty nice entertainer around town. We played at some places on Nineteenth and Twentieth Streets. We used to get together there and do some sounds, but not too much. We'd get into those places where alcohol and water was, and there'd be a piano or something in there, and I'd pick guitar with him.

Barrelhouse Buck was even harder to work with than Walter Davis — and you know how Walter Davis played off. For another musician to play with Walter was a very hard task because he made his own thing his own way. He didn't have no nothing, just whatever. He inserted his feelings in his music at all times. Buck was something like Walter or worse. When you work on your own you can do what you wanna do. I'm guilty of that quite a bit, fixing it just like I want it to be.

Now Buck and Peetie Wheatstraw was together quite a bit. I don't know if they ever recorded together or not, but they kinda come along together.[25] I've seen them play together. If Peetie Wheatstraw was playing, Buck would make an effort to work with him, and that would change it up some. Wheatstraw would play guitar with Buck. They had some similar styles they played. Buck's was more of a drive beat sound, and Peetie Wheatstraw had a kind of rhythm riff with his. But there was a medium in there where they both done somewhat the same thing, the little turnaround. Buck would just quit playing piano and his hand would just go to beating on the piano, bom, bom, bom. That was one of his barrelhouse kickoffs, his typical style. He done it with class — it fitted what he was doing. That was Barrelhouse Buck's trademark. Buck finally left the city and went up in Alton, Illinois, someplace.

I knew Peetie Wheatstraw pretty well, not as buddy-buddies or nothing like that, but we associated frequently together. Around at these houses and things we'd do some sounds together and what have you. He wound up living here in the city, and I read a lot where they claim an East St. Louis deal. I think he lived in St. Louis for a longer period of time than he did in East St. Louis. Of course he lived in East St. Louis also. Wheatstraw played both piano and guitar depending on who he was with and where he was at. And sometimes he would do both, but I would have to say that he played more guitar than piano because he didn't always find a piano.

I never knew Wheatstraw to go out of town to work — no further than East St. Louis. He'd work over on Third Street and at a place out in Brooklyn, Illinois. He worked all over East St. Louis. Peetie had become very famous, but I never did know him to take a tour. Back in that time there wasn't too much of this promotion. When I was out there with Roosevelt, there wasn't nobody handling us, we were just on our own. Peetie was doing just about as well here as he would anywhere else. Around town he was pretty well busy, his name was ringing.

Peetie Wheatstraw used to work periodically with a fellow name Neckbones — his name was Willie something, but we called him Neckbones.[26] He was a good guitar player — good and fast — and I understand he recorded with Wheatstraw. I've no knowledge of where Neckbones came from — I've never heard this mentioned. He was an elder man than me, he must have had me by eight or ten years. Wheatstraw was older than me. See, when I was a kid, they were men, and I know that. I called myself a man along with them, but I wasn't, and I know they were.

The first time I met Memphis Minnie was down on Division Street at Neckbones's house. I didn't know her reason for being in St. Louis at that time, but a friend of mine name Tobe Williams, who was a close associate of Neckbones, come and got me to let me know she was here. After that I saw her quite a few times down through the years.

At the time of Peetie Wheatstraw's death, he and Walter Davis were about the most popular people.[27] They were the two most famous people in the city of St. Louis. Walter had made the "M and O Blues" and Peetie was in his bloom. I think Henry Spaulding had passed on then, because he wasn't in that ring. He was there part of the time, then he disappeared out of it. So I'm thinking Spaulding, he died somewhere in the 1930s.

It was a big thing when Peetie Wheatstraw died. A lot of people took that pretty hard. The St. Louis newspapers may not have carried the story — they were less interested in what Peetie Wheatstraw was doing than anything you would ever imagine. It wasn't anything for them to even think about, the death wasn't even important.

Black newspapers didn't even carry it, much less the whites. But if you wanted to find out when he was arrested, you could find that out. They got a record of him on that, I bet you, probably a pretty long one. I bet they got records on him if he did or didn't commit anything. He got arrested plenty. Being a musician, how could you avoid it? They cooked up something on him regardless of what he was doing. Gambling or doing something. They wouldn't just say he's playing music, because there would be no need for them to arrest him.

I knew Jabo Williams from down on Biddle Street, and I played guitar behind Jabo Williams around town here. Jabo didn't devote a whole lot of his time into piano. Jabo was more or less in the hustling bracket, just like the McKnights were. Occasionally he would get on the piano and play for his own entertainment or for some little jump-up thing. But to get engaged to play someplace — I don't think Jabo ever went out for that, as good as he was. If it come up a half-assed thing, he'd get on the piano and do his thing and that would be it. But where's the crap game? Or where's the card game? He was a hustler and a gambler.

Jabo was an average guy and he was very entertaining. He liked to talk quite a bit. He was a pretty good piano player, but he wasn't quite raised up as good as Roosevelt Sykes or Henry Brown. Jabo also had a brother name Sambo — his name was Samuel, but we called him Sambo. He would bang on the piano a little bit, but he never did come up to anything. Jabo recorded, but he wasn't around too long after that. He disappeared from St. Louis and went down in Arkansas someplace. I never knew what the hell had happened to him. This was probably in the top of the thirties. He may have been around before I knew him, but he wasn't around too long after I got to know him.[28]

There was also another guy that was an extremely good piano player, and he was employed at some of the places — we called him Lay 'Em Straight. I didn't know of any other name, just that one. Henry Brown, Roosevelt, and Lay 'Em Straight were extreme piano players in the blues field around here at that time. Lay 'Em Straight was a very famous piano player around here. He never recorded, but he kind of had prestige over this boy, "I'm So Glad I'm Twenty-one Years Old," Joe Dean. Pete Bogans would kind of associate with him.

Pete Bogans would also work quite a bit on guitar with Pinetop Sparks. The first place I knew Pinetop Sparks to play at was Nettie's on Delmar. It was a basement, a sizable place about the 2600 or 2800 block on Delmar. He was at Nettie's for the longest period of time — from the time I knew him until he expired he was there. Between Nettie's, Charley Houston's, and a few other spots — the speakeasy type places — most of us would be in and out of them kind of places.

Pinetop's mother and father lived on the corner of Seventh and Wash. His sister Jimmie Lee also sang — she was one of the best in St. Louis. She didn't record, but she was better than Alice Moore. She was beautiful. She sang mostly with Pinetop, Pete Bogans played guitar, and Ike Rogers played trombone. Sometimes this fellow Sam played trumpet — he was also great. He'd draw a crowd just by himself, no support, no nothing. Pinetop's brother Lindberg picked up all of his singing from his sister Jimmie Lee. She never was discovered. It's a shame — all of that talent went to waste.

Milton Sparks killed somebody one time, but it was in defense of his own life.[29] Bootlegging, alcohol charges, and all of that, those kind of things were sometimes exaggerated. Let me say it this way: if you appear to be a renowned person and black in the city of St. Louis, they piled up everything they could against you to stop you from being influenceable. They done that religiously with everybody they could do it with. And Pinetop and Lindberg's name began to sound around the city, so they started piling things up. Believe it or not, they got me charged with a lot of things that I didn't do. They got me two or three times for weapons, and I ain't seen one yet. I don't know nothing about it, but it's down there against me.

Pinetop had a very gentle nature: he seemed to be friendly with everybody and he was easy to make friends with and he was a floater with women. You couldn't hardly make the man mad about nothing, contrary to how his brother was. He was real good-natured, and so was his sister. Pinetop and Lindberg didn't work together a whole lot, just occasionally. Lindberg worked with other people more than he did Pinetop. They didn't see eye to eye at all times. They were ordinary brothers, agreeing to disagree.

But Pinetop was just night and day. I know this fellow would play on weekends — Friday, Saturday, and possibly Sunday — and he was the type of guy who didn't use the word *no* too often. He would be with one crowd all night, a fresh crowd would come and get him in the morning, and another crowd in the evening. He was good for losing twenty-four hours' sleep on the weekends, and this is what they claimed he died of. Now drinking was also a part of that, because this was an artificial fight-back against staying up. He would fall asleep, but as soon as they could get him revived, he was right back in there again. He just done burned himself out. I also had experience with that. I know exactly how it goes. I never knew until then that you can get to the place where you can't sleep. The doctors said that Pinetop was something like six months behind in his rest, and they couldn't bring him back around.

I first met Henry Brown way back in the 1920s — he and Ike Rogers was together at that time.[30] I knew him before he first recorded. I never done any recording with him, but I worked with him in clubs and whatnot. Pete Bogans also worked with him too. Henry Brown would also work solo, but in most cases he and Ike Rogers was a team. You see one, you see the other: Brown on piano and Ike on trombone. Mary Johnson also sang with Henry Brown quite a bit, more than anybody else.

Brown was a more level guy than Roosevelt, more smooth. He was a very decent fellow, very easygoing. The one hitch Brown had was he didn't know when to let the bottle loose; he would hold it until it got him. Outside of that there's nothing at all in there that you can say about Brown. I guess I was the last person to work with him on anything he done. That's my old buddy.

five

"THE MUSIC IS A MIND DISTURBER"

I've had some ups and downs in my life, like everybody else. I know my first wife gave me a really tough time. I don't know the date I married her, but I know I was twenty-five years old. Her name was Florence McKinnon. Was it McKinnon or McKinley? Ain't that something? We met at John M. Hawkins's place. She came down there with another fellow, James Morris was his name — I think that's who she was fiddling around with at the time. I really don't know how we got together. I remember one thing: I asked her about moving pictures and we got into conversation on that. Anyway, we went to see a movie, and as we were walking back from the movie this guy that she'd been seeing had an automobile, and he drove by. He saw us and he called, and she wouldn't go to him, and he drove on off. And from then on it was her and me.

We never had any children; she was never able to carry. She'd start out but was never able to make it. She was doing private family work, laundry, and whatever come up. We stayed together a pretty good while, about ten years. But she turned out to be not such a good person. She was all right, but as time went along she began to get jealous, and a jealous person can't be exactly what they should be. They always feel that you're doing something — and for God's sake they always want revenge.

They do what they think you're doing in order to get even with you. And you're not doing anything of the kind. The truth is, she would go out and get all tore down drinking. Many times I'd be home in bed and she'd come home and deliberately jump on me. I went along with it for a long time. One time I was laying in the bed and we was talking, and all of a sudden she hauls off and bangs me with a shoe right in my head — one of them old tall shoes — and boy, did that hurt. So I didn't go along with it that time. I had to grease her up a little bit! I gave her one of them extraordinary spankings. That started the wheel to rolling; as long as she was beating up on me it was all right, but when I retaliated, things changed. We didn't hold on too long after that.

She would play a lot of tricks on me. I remember one specific thing that she done when she wanted to get out. You've heard the song Walter Davis sang: "she called the law on me for no reason and had me locked up." I found out later what that was about. That was a trend amongst black women at that time. They could holler "police," and the police would come and arrest you with no evidence whatsoever. She could just say I was threatening to whoop her, and they would come and take you away. The police come and arrested me, then I was good for that amount of hours down there. And whatever she wanted to do, she had plenty of time to have her fun and do it. This was the first time she had done that to me, but that was one time too many.

Eventually she left. I remained where I was, but I wouldn't let her back. Oh, she wanted to come back, but I refused. I knew that was out and over, the one that broke the camel's back. We finally got divorced when I came out of the service in 1945, and that closed the deal on that particular thing.

In the mid-1930s I was living at 2320 Carr Street — there's a school sitting there now. Anyway, I got into the bootlegging, alcohol and water business then. A lady who rented my basement actually started me doing that. She was on her own with three kids, and after a while she got a job down at a place called the Brown Mule, which I think was down on Seventh Street. Whiskey had just come in at this time.[1] She'd bring home bottles of whiskey and she had that basement stocked, and a lot of it was sealed bottles. She said they were working her to death and not paying her anything, so she was stealing. Well, I wasn't too fond of that, but I couldn't tell her what to do. She wanted me to sell the stuff and split it with her, so I said okay. I also had alcohol and water there as well, but the guys wanted that better drink; it was more money and I had what they wanted.

That went on for quite some time, but I got a little shaky over it, so I got me a place across the alley, and nobody come in or out not knowing me. Money was coming in real fast and I helped her to get herself good and started.

Well, the news started to get around, and the law enforcement started to come around, but they could never catch nothing on me — I handled that real good. Matter of fact, I never did really have anything there to amount to anything. If they come to the door I'd only have one or two — and I didn't have no problem getting rid of that.

One time a policeman come in and said, "I know you're selling whiskey. Don't you want to give us a little something? I tell you what you do, you give me a drink, give me a half-pint."

I said, "I'll get you a half-pint, wait 'til I get back." So I went on out the back door — I could go through the gangways from my house over to Franklin. There was a cigar store there at that time at Jefferson and Franklin, and they had package liquor and whatnot, so I picked up a half-pint and brought it back to the house.

He looked at it, the stamp was on it: "Townsend, you think you're slick."

I said, "You said you wanted a half-pint. I told you I'd get you one. If you don't want it, leave it here. I'll sell it to somebody."

He said, "I know you're selling whiskey."

I said, "I'm gonna sell this because you told me to go get it and I don't want it." So he sat there and drink the half-pint and he tried to bribe me into telling him some of this and some of that. I had nothing to tell him, and they didn't actually bother me again.

I also bought whiskey from Scarfino and a guy down on Thirteenth Street, in the alley between Biddle and Carr, called B. B. He was another Italian down in there, he was a wholesale man. He handled five-gallon cans of alcohol. Those were the people, you know, you better watch where you buy — some of them had reputations. Some of them had poison and stuff out there killing people, so you had to watch what you do. But these people that I'm speaking of, they didn't have that kind of a problem; they were pretty good.

I also had music at my place and I'd do my own sounds in there. That's where I'd draw a crowd at — people could ball all night at my house. At the time Ernest Walker had a place two doors from me. A confectionery was there and his house was also up there, but he didn't stay there. He had one of his gals running the house and she sold bootleg stuff too. We both knew what was happening and we'd help one another out. I would also go down to his house and play, and that's where I first got with this buddy of mine who also played guitar, Joe Harding. He never did do no recording, but he played with me all over town. He lived at Ernest Walker's a while, then he moved to Detroit.

Ernest Walker and I kinda come along together, and at one time we roomed together on Delmar. He was a hustler and a loan shark and eventually one of his buddies killed him. He also had a house that he used for a joint on Jefferson, between Biddle and Division, and that's where I met Robert Johnson at.[2]

Ernest knew him by some means, and he had gotten a hold of him, as he was there by request. I was there playing, and he and I was supposed to take turns and work. People were very much concerned with his gift of playing; he had undivided attention when he'd be playing. I liked his finger style as well as I liked his slide style. He done more slide when I was there with him, because we was playing together.

The first few nights he was over there, he was doing his own thing and I was doing mine. He would do as much finger work as he would slide work, then when I start playing with him he went to exclusive slide. He really had some sweet, sweet sounds, some sweet chords he'd make. You don't hear too many people doing it. I found myself doing some of it, but I didn't want to adapt myself towards it — I didn't want to mix it with mine. It would have been too much work to integrate it with my sounds.

To me Robert Johnson was an average kind of guy. He was quiet — he'd talk to you if you talk, he wasn't gonna increase the conversation. He'd answer questions you'd ask the quickest way he could and get through with it. He wasn't like I've heard people say — he wasn't women crazy at all. He didn't pay the women no more attention than he did the men. All the gals were like they were to every other musician: they were breakin' down, but it didn't seem to go to his head.

I think Robert Johnson had out "Terraplane Blues" or something like that then.[3] He also played out there at this little place called Future City, out from Cairo. He was out there a few times. I happened to be down there visiting my cousin who lived in Future City, but I didn't get to see Robert there. But this was when that record was hot. He was just kinda going through the country firing up.

But there was plenty of other people before and after Robert Johnson. In his time, like everything else, he was it. But that don't stay forever. Nothing is forever. Nothing is for all time that is created, especially by man. Maybe by God it's for all times forever, but not by man.

I first met Charley Jordan when he was living on Seventeenth Street right near Cole Street. A lady from Cairo whose relatives I knew started rooming with Charley, and they got to be lovers. I went to visit the lady, and that's where I first met him. This was before any recording was done by him or me, way before the recording, before I was even playing guitar. But he was playing guitar. I considered Charley an older man as of then; he must have been in his thirties good or maybe forties. Charley was a paraplegic; he was crippled, paralyzed from the waist down. He had no use of it at all, but his upper body functioned normally.

I never knew Charley to have another occupation other than music. I would guess that he was getting aid from the state before he started making money from his music — I couldn't see how else he would survive other than that. Charley was a good guitar player. I highly respected his guitar playing because he could accompany anybody. Piano, another guitar player, or what have you, he was qualified to back it up.

When Charley got into music he was full-time with it. He had people every day rehearsing, trying to put packages together, week in and week out. Sometimes it would be months, maybe a year before they recorded, but they'd be there every day.[4] He had a little organized club with people paying membership that would support him in his expense for lights, etc. I was in and out of there, but I can't quite place its locations; it was either Tenth, Eleventh, or Twelfth Streets, in the Biddle Street neighborhood. I'm also reasonably sure he picked himself up some money by selling liquor — that was a kinda boost to his livelihood. Peetie Wheatstraw was one of the persons that he recommended, and of course that gave him a little leverage, because Peetie was red hot for a long time. So the record companies started to look at Charley with some kind of respect. He had people coming from everywhere rehearsing, trying to pass the test for a recording session, because he was the sole judge of that for a while, the scout.

I've been asked a thousand times, "Who was 'Hi' Henry Brown?" I don't know! I've got ideas, but I can't say I know. But I'm a firm believer that Charley Jordan is "Hi" Henry Brown. All of the names that done anything in the city of St. Louis I was familiar with — it wasn't a broad thing where there were so many musicians here we didn't know half of them, wasn't no such thing as that. If anybody was doing anything at all, we all knew, and the people that was there in the time that this thing come out, well I would have known, there's no doubt about it.[5] But that one number, "Nut Factory," there was a nut factory at Sixteenth and Delmar that specialized in nuts, mostly pecans.[6] I think it was Charley Jordan. I don't know why, but there's a lot of thing that connect me with Charley Jordan and this song. I hear quite a bit of his voice and his style in that song.

Now Lane Hardin was one of the least know musicians around the city, because he had come into the city and hadn't exposed himself much. He had a job at Lewins Metal Company and hadn't been exposed by his music until he ran across Wheatstraw's buddy, Neckbones, who also worked over there. They got to talking and found out about playing music, and that's how he got to be discovered. They would meet at different houses and just do something for their own personal entertainment, but not for jobs that I know of. Lane Hardin also played out at McKnight's place in Kinloch. Lane could have been slightly older than me, but not by much. He lived on Biddle Street about Thirteenth or Fourteenth — they had built a little row of new houses, and he lived there. I never met a wife, but he had a girlfriend that lived across the street.[7]

After Lane Hardin had done his recording, he continued to work over at Lewins.[8] I think he worked there until they closed down or a very short time before they closed — he'd been there for some time. I even worked over there for a short spell, and when I say a short spell I mean one day. That wasn't cut out for me; there was too much smoke and those people inhaled that stuff. I went in there and done that day — I wanted to see exactly what it was about. I stayed with it that day but never did return. I don't even know if I returned for my pay. This was the latter part of the 1930s, and to the best of my knowledge that plant closed in the last of the 1940s or early 1950s.

At one recording session we met Leroy Carr and Scrapper Blackwell — I couldn't forget that because at that time both of these people were my choice in music; they were idols to me. I was beginning to try and branch away from Lonnie Johnson's style a little and do Scrapper's style — all that heavy bass work, picking guitar. I would never forget those two people. I was a great admirer of Leroy Carr, how unconcerned he could play piano, just like he wasn't doing anything at all. He'd be working with so much effortless moves. I think they came in the studio that morning and concluded their session that same morning, and we come in the afternoon to do ours. They were taking down as we coming in.[9]

Everything Leroy was making for a while was pretty popular, that "How Long" and "Prison Bound," just about everything — he was pretty hot.[10] He was the hottest thing going then. I saw them one more time after that, but they wasn't together. I was visiting St. Louis Jimmy in Indianapolis when he stayed over there, and I run into Leroy. It wasn't at no club or nothing, just around. And I also met Scrapper — that must've been in Indianapolis too, but not at the same time. I had a conversation with him, but the first time we got acquainted was in the studio. I know I met Leroy with Jimmy. Roosevelt Sykes also stayed over there for a while with Jimmy.

St. Louis Jimmy and me used to bum around quite a bit. I met Jimmy back in the 1920s out at the Hodiamont Tracks. Streetcars used to run up there and houses lined up and down the tracks. This was out around Hamilton Avenue; all of this is destroyed now, but it ran in the alley, and the tracks are still in the alley. The area was extremely far west of downtown, but that particular section is where blacks lived, and that's where St. Louis Jimmy was staying.[11]

Jimmy and I used to hang out over there on Fairfax; we would be there daily. There were places over there to play where they would just create a party. Jimmy had a brother that worked for a contracting company that hauled cement. He drove one of their trucks, and that was a good-paying job. Most of the places we'd be partying at sold alcohol, and he'd often stop off and set the house up or leave two or three dollars with Jimmy. We'd blow that drinking it up. That was all I could drink because the stuff only cost ten or fifteen cents a half-pint. We's also go over in the Ville quite a bit, over on Newstead and Garfield — one of the places was over there.

St. Louis Jimmy wasn't too much of a piano player, but he had a couple of numbers that he could do. But I don't think he ever recorded with his own backup. He took engagements and he'd go around where different piano players were or he'd be hired where different piano players were for his vocal ability. I know he worked with Roosevelt quite a bit and I understand he also worked with Lonnie Johnson too. But he was a good songwriter, no doubt about it. He could get a subject and work with it real decent.

When Jimmy left St. Louis he was kind of wanted a little bit. There was a guy that had a little old Ford pickup truck, and Jimmy would sometimes drive for him. Jimmy would also use the truck with the consent of the owner. One night Jimmy and Roosevelt were drinking and they decided that they wanted to go somewhere, and Jimmy went and got the truck without the consent of the man. The man missed the truck and put the call out. They were fortunate enough to get away from the truck and not get caught, but the pressure was on. I guess they didn't want to come in contact with the law, so they both split town. Roosevelt went on to Chicago and Jimmy checked out a little while. Eventually he decided he would go there too, and I know a year didn't expire before he come out with this "Going Down Slow."[12]

People have passed on, and the streets they lived on have done passed on. I was thinking about Blind Darby — the guitar player Teddy Darby — and Tommy Webb, his piano player. They're both dead and the streets they lived on ain't there no more. Division is gone and of course Short Market is gone.

Tommy Webb was a reasonably good piano player. If he was at liberty to execute his own style, it was a style that would touch upon Leroy Carr's a little bit. Him and Darby were also supposed to be relatives — cousins — and he accompanied Darby most of the time. They played periodically in a lot of the clubs and places where everybody else played, except the big-time clubs. They would play at these house parties, like Charley Houston's place, Betty and Molly's place, and Sadie's, which was down on Delmar. It was also called the Hole in the Ground. Pinetop also used to play there.

Blind Darby was a nut. He was blind and he was a jealous musician and he was jealous of his ladies, which I guess was a miserable life — couldn't see and being jealous. And he was sort of treacherous as a blind man. He hurt several people — he cut up several people — and he could be dangerous. He developed the sense that blind people have, and sound was his eyes. But it would seem like where there was two or three people, he would get the sounds kind of scrambled and wouldn't know who was who. Not so. They are sensitive to certain sounds; nature builds it in some kinda way, your walk don't sound like another guy's.

I saw a case where him and some fellow got into it, and the guy eased away without making a sound and got around behind another guy. And the other man walked right on past Darby, and he knew it wasn't him. And when this other guy started over towards him, Darby come up with his knife, and his cousin had to stop him. He knew exactly where that guy was at all time if he made a sound. Well, that frightened me. I was scared that he might not know my sound and come after me. So I dismissed me. Every time he would get into one of them moods, if I was there, I'd no longer be around.

* * *

I guess I make Big Joe Williams a whipping boy, but he's one of the guys that the less you listen to him, the better off you are when you start talking about things. Big Joe would cool if there was somebody around that knows quite a bit, but if there wasn't, he fixed it his way. Big Joe and me done a lot of things in the studio and a few things around the city of St. Louis, but most of that was around my house.[13]

We never did do no clubs together and all of this kind of a thing. It's been written where we played together in East St. Louis — I don't remember them times.

I think Big Joe is one of the guys that said Walter Davis played in nightclubs and things. Walter never did do nothing like that. He didn't do no entertaining, not to my knowledge, none whatsoever. Walter was too bashful, number one. After he got so he wasn't studio shy, he was fine; but out there in the public, no. I don't think Walter thought of himself as a musician to play in the public. I've seen it in print where he's played at such and such a club; not so. Walter was very, very bashful when it came to public entertainment, and his wasn't that kind of entertaining music. I've never known him to be booked on no job, not even no house party.

Walter used to have a gal named Mary he used to live with, and she had a piano, and he used to practice and go on with that. Maybe somebody would come there and he'd play something. This was in his early days, when he was just learning to play, and he wasn't playing all that good. This was before he went to work at the hotel. After he got his start with Roosevelt, all he would do was record. Walter ain't played in no club nowhere.

Walter Davis played some of the saddest songs that was ever heard about. I think he was thinking right, because he knew this wouldn't draw a crowd. Each one of them would get up and get them a bat, go home, and go to fighting or do something. A gal would go home and get the rolling pin and go to hitting someone over the head.

To me Walter had experienced a whole lot for somebody his age — about how the world is, about people, and the just or unjust that was being done amongst couples. Look like to me he had a whole lot of experience with that. He could go very deep into the matters that people bring up against one another, and that was amazing to me. He really pulled me into it in a sense, the same things that way.

He could tell some of the saddest stories 'bout two people who were supposed to be in agreement. From my viewpoint he could tell stories sadder than anybody I know. The music is a mind disturber — the man puts you back into thoughts that you didn't want to entertain. Not good time. He'd be telling that story about the guy like Poor Kelly. Say,

"I know they gonna get me, / gonna send me to the electric chair, / but I don't care." That's the kind of music Walter played.

Walter was the type of guy that would actually think thoroughly before he made any announcements. He spoke slowly, but he would comb everything through before he would come up with any kind of a decision. When he spoke, he would stop at intervals as though he wasn't sure he should say this or maybe he should say something else. He was a very particular guy about what he said. He would think twice before he speak.

Walter's parents lived 1900 something on Biddle Street and he also had a little ice cream parlor business going on at the time. It wasn't a big thing, but he could live out of it for sure. He was also a very handsome-looking man, and the gals took over. I know this one woman that lived down on Carr Street was pretty wealthy — her and her mother owned the finest building down there — and she went nuts over Walter, and Walter let her. If her and Walter would go someplace and Walter would happen to see something, she'd get it for him without him even asking her. But he wouldn't let her do some of the things she wanted to do because she wanted too much of his time.

There was rumor that got twisted around that Walter had killed someone in Chicago. He killed a man, but it wasn't in Chicago; it was right in St. Louis down on Biddle Street. Walter was living with his mother and father at the time, and there was a tavern on the corner of the next street, which was Twentieth Street, and that's where this occurred. This man killed himself — that's the way Walter put it when he killed him. And he did.

The guy's name was Willie White, and he thought Walter was bothering his woman, and it wasn't him at all.[14] But this guy thought it was, and he went to picking at Walter about it. Walter explained himself to him that it wasn't him, but the guy wouldn't let that do. Somebody else was going with the girl; she lived across the street from Walter. He didn't drink, he'd only go down to the tavern to socialize with some people he knew. Occasionally the girl would also go in there, and one time the guy came in there and she was sitting down talking to Walter.

And this was the first time the boy clowned and went off. So Walter told him, "Man, I ain't got your woman." The woman wasn't in Walter's company no more, but he couldn't settle for that. He broke at Walter one time, and somebody grabbed him and held him and Walter told him, "Man you gonna keep on, you're gonna kill yourself. Keep on making them charges at me, you're gonna kill yourself."

Sure enough, Walter was in the tavern one night sitting down, and the guy walked in there, spied Walter, and pulled out his knife and broke for him. Walter come up with that .38. The guy saw that .38 and went to run out the door. But it was too late then — Walter wouldn't let him get away; he turned it loose on him.

This boy didn't know it, but Walter was carrying a gold badge then which allowed him to carry a pistol. Walter had also reported to the commander in chief downtown about this guy threatening him and asked him what would be the way out. The man told him, "If you can manage to hold him and call us, do that. But if you can't, do what you have to do." I think they had it set up down there — you know how it goes down: if he does it again, just go on and kill him. I don't think Walter really wanted to kill him, because he did warn him, but the guy came up with it again. I think he threatened Walter three times. Anyway, it was almost over before it got started. The department was aware of it, and you know how simple it would be for them to clear it up. They write it off just like writing off tax.

We'd also ride freight trains. Walter didn't have no Cadillac then — this was before that, before he went to work at the hotel. This was when his hit come out.[15] Sometimes I'd go by and tell him, "Well, I'm fittin' to leave town." He'd say, "Where you going, Mule?" "I don't know, I'm just gonna grab me a train." He'd say, "Wait a minute, I'll get dressed." He'd go and put on a suit and some coveralls and put them on — we kept them for our traveling. We'd go down in New Madrid, Missouri, Cairo, Illinois, and sometimes we'd go to Peoria, Illinois. Sometimes we'd make a round trip — just ride away and ride back. I'd take my guitar; that was my bread ticket.

Walter would never play no place, except one job he had down in his home town, New Madrid, and we went down there and played. He went down to see his mother — this was before his parents moved to St. Louis. Walter was out from Mississippi first, but they migrated to New Madrid, Missouri.[16] Now I forgot the man's name, but he lived across the road from his mother on a little farm. He had a little week-end thing that he carried on, and Walter and I played for them.

This was also the first time we got into an argument. He told me, "Listen, you think you're kinda tough."

I said, "No, I think you're the one that think you're kinda tough."

Walter said, "You think you can whoop me?"

I said, "No, I think you're the one that thinks you can whoop me." We were talking like that.

So he said, "Well" — he had a funny way he'd go "ha-ha" — "Well, we're gonna try."

I said, "For what?"

"We're gonna find out if I can whoop you and you can whoop me."

I said, "Walter, I hate that you want to do it that way, and you got the best of it."

He said, "Why?"

I said, "There your brother is, and there ain't nobody but me."

He said, "I can get my brother to stay out of it; it won't be nobody but me and you."

I said, "Then I'm gonna have to accept your challenge."

Him and I went together and we had a pretty good round. I think the thing come out pretty well, even from my viewpoint. I crippled him up pretty bad and he done me in pretty bad and we called it off and declared it no ill feelings. But I was disgusted, and I asked him just why did he want to carry on like that. He said he just thought he could whoop me. I said that I didn't think that he could whoop me, but I knew I wasn't gonna let him whoop me! So we called it off.

When we got ready to leave there we caught a train, and the old brakeman spotted us and he was determined to make us get off the train. Well, I had as much experience riding trains as he did, because at that time I rode the railroad just about all over the States. He attempted to catch us down between the cars, and when he come to find us, we'd climbed to the other side. He started from the caboose and we made our way almost to the coal tender, then we'd climb down. Then we'd come back up middle ways in the train. Now here he comes. It takes a little time to run that train when it's moving because it's wobbling. Then we'd get down between the cars, get the stirrups, maybe get on the coupling and go back under the side, and he'd go on by us. Well, you can't ride down there too long, because when the train picks up speed, those cinders and things whoop you to death.

Now by the time he gets down to the caboose and gets settled, we're back on top. That was puzzling to him, so I told Walter, "I tell you what we do: just let him catch us and instead of us getting off, maybe he'll have to get off."

So Walter said, "That's a good idea, Mule."

So he comes up there and asked us what the hell we think we were doing, and we were gonna have to get off. I said, "No. Now you're gonna have to think about that good. If you want somebody off here, you better go over there and jump off, because we're going on over to Cairo."

He said, "You know it's against the law?"

I said, "Yeah, that's understood, but give a little consideration and don't try and make nobody get off."

He said, "Well, you're gonna have to get off."

I said, "I'm sorry you said that, because you're gonna have to get off."

So Walter said, "You climb down now." So the guy climbed down — we didn't make him jump off though. After a while he come back up and went on back to the caboose. About that time, train was coming across the bridge into Cairo and we got off.

Another time we was on the road just hoboing around, and we got off a train somewhere in southern Illinois near Carbondale, down that way. Anyway, we was just browsing around in the little old town, and we heard about a place for entertainment, and that's where we saw a "Walter Davis and Henry" entertaining. Now "Walter Davis" had pictures out, and he didn't favor Walter no kind of way — I didn't know how he thought that he was getting away with it. He could play something similar, but not too much. And the guitar player was a thousand miles from where he ought to have been being "Henry." He had some good sounds that he could play, but they wasn't really too good together. We just laughed about it, had fun about it, and went on and left the guys with whoever they thought they were. We never bothered it, we let "Walter Davis and Henry" stay there and play. Now maybe this would help explain the reason why it was said that Walter

Davis had played in clubs and things, because there were imitators out there. Walter Davis never played in no clubs, take it from me.

After Walter moved out of his mother's house, he moved into the hotel, and that's how he come into the job there. He was earning good money working at the hotel and his Cadillac come from the hotel. He worked at the Calumet Hotel first — he worked there for years and years. Then he went to the West End Hotel, and after that he come out on Page Avenue to the Albany Hotel, and that's where his illness struck him down at, at the Albany. He didn't have much time out because it was an eight day a week job, twenty-four hours a day.[17]

Walter Davis never did cease recording. He recorded pretty well up to his contract. The amount of times he was supposed to be called, he was pretty well there each time. And he had the most decent contract that I know — he was never hungry. Walter was never hungry since he left East St. Louis and he made that first record.

Walter relied on me at first because he knew he wasn't good enough with his piano. And down through the years he still relied on me to take care of his mistakes, and I did a pretty good job of it, I think. Later on as he began to record with the piano himself, he didn't need no takin' care of; he could take care of himself. He progressed with the piano pretty fast.[18]

I met Lester Melrose several times but I never did deal with him direct. He never did record me. He asked me about ten times to record, but me and him never could see eye to eye on nothing. He went as far as to ask me, "Well, why do you play for people and get far less than I'm gonna pay you?" I said, "Because I'm not doing for them what I'd be doing for you."[19]

On sessions I worked with Walter, I was working for Walter. Everything was agreed upon by Walter Davis, and we had an agreement at that time. We had another agreement with the transportation, and I was the transportation man. Melrose, of course, paid Walter. I don't know what Big Joe and them had with him. Big Joe and Nighthawk probably could have been with Melrose, but it was Walter and I. Melrose never dealt with me. But I think I had just set my mind against doing anything for him. Nothing he would say would enthuse me at all.

At one time Walter Davis sued RCA and got a settlement; I think Walter got quite a bit, and he was doing pretty well in royalties off "M and O Blues." In fact, I think he hit RCA twice. He hit them once because they hadn't given him some royalties, and I think a lawyer advised him to hit them again for recording a minor. At that time this would stand up in court real strong, if you wasn't twenty-one. This was in the 1940s.[20] Walter always used to claim that he was older than me, and we was betting and going on. So one day we was up to his mama's house there on Biddle Street, and his mother gave his date of birth as 1909. His brother Willie was younger than him.[21]

I recorded at a couple of places in Illinois for Bluebird, in Chicago and Aurora, and right around the lake out of Chicago in Wisconsin for Paramount. We also recorded in Louisville, Kentucky — that trip was done with Jesse Johnson. And Walter and I went to Nashville, Tennessee, to record for Bullet.[22] But I don't recall any studio set up in St. Louis doing any recording at any time, except way back when I wasn't too much into the music field, when the Starr Piano Company was in St. Louis.

Walter and I was also together when "Tears Come Rollin' Down" was written, and I had him in mind to do just what was done, to do the vocal. He had to continue with his style to make it as good as it could be, and that was satisfactory — it worked out pretty good.[23] My wife Vernell fell in love with it years later and she insisted on doing it, so I let her do it.

But here's the way "Tears Come Rollin' Down" first was: "Although she kissed me, / I still knew she was leaving town." Neither one of us don't go with that now, but that was the way it was written. I go with "kiss me good night" and Vernell went with something else. Walter sang it the way Vernell done it. He switched it around a little bit. He said he forgot the words to it — it was all right to. The song suited him, and as he was the one doing the vocals, so what else was there to do? It was his privilege to do that. If he had put more words in it, it would have crowded his style. He was pretty warm at that time, and I figured he would be more likely to push it further than I would. That song paid me some pretty good money outside of the session.

✳ ✳ ✳

I think it was Big Joe Williams who was the one that caused Sonny Boy Williamson and I to meet. He brought him to my house when I was living at 1308 Euclid Avenue, and Sonny Boy stayed with me for about a week. Lacy Belle, his wife, wasn't with him at this time. I don't know if he was married to her then or he was just courting her, but that was all his conversation was about when you get to talking, Lacy Belle. He also had some kin people in St. Louis, some cousins and so on.

He played up in houses, anywhere he could, but I don't know of any regular engagements that Sonny Boy ever got here — he would muscle his way in on everything. If he wanted to play across town, he'd wait until evening and go in one of them places and take him a job, and he was accepted — that's the way he would do it. He was also one of the only guys that I know that could go to the job with a harmonica by himself. He walk in on his own and take him a job and they would accept him.

At first he was just playing acoustic harmonica, and somehow that acoustic harmonica was good enough — a reasonable size crowd could hear it. The places that he worked at could hear it, and that was good enough. Later on he got an amp; I think he picked him up an amp about the same time Joe Williams got one. Joe had one of them old-time square tin boxes. But Sonny Boy never did really live here, he would just come and stay here with friends.[24]

Sonny Boy and Big Joe come to my house one time and we done some playing. I don't remember exactly what it was now, but something went contrary to what Big Joe wanted to do and I had to get him out of there — he wanted to do Sonny Boy in. He pulled his knife and he would cut you — don't think he wouldn't. I don't understand it, but Big Joe always did respect me in a certain way.

Sonny Boy was, well, not quite an ordinary guy. He was kinda loud when he'd be drinking. I wouldn't call him an overbearing guy, but he would speak up for himself without any hesitation. He wasn't a belligerent type of guy, but he was pretty strong-minded. And he had very high self-esteem; he thought quite a bit of himself.

I kind of gave myself some credit for getting along with the guys that nobody could get along with. I never did have any problem with them. And it wasn't because I'd bend over for them, it was just because of the way I carried myself with them. Sonny Boy wasn't an easy guy to get along with, and Big Joe Williams most certainly was not, if you were a musician. But I never had any trouble out of any of them.

I first met Big Joe Williams way back in the 1930s. He was living on Twenty-second Street off Franklin Avenue. He was living with a woman named Mamie then, who kept house for some white people, and she would come home on the weekends. Joe was about the only musician around St. Louis that had a pretty good little old amplifier. I believe it was an old Webco. He wasn't playing nine-string guitar then, he was playing a regular guitar. Later on he added one string, then another, then another.

Big Joe was also one of the most jealous musicians you've ever seen in your life. One time we were doing a show in St. Louis and he wouldn't play — they couldn't get him up on the stage. I told them, "I can get him up there. Set the piano up and I'll get to playing and announce that Henry Townsend is doing Big Joe's session, and I'll bet you he'll come up."

They did that and I started to playing and Big Joe went, "What the hell is he doing up there? It's my time!"

So they said, "Well Joe, you said you wasn't gonna play for no son-of-a-bitch."

He said, "Well that's all right. I'm going up there!"

Joe drank. He couldn't hold his whiskey, and he felt a little less than he should have felt about himself. He didn't have the feeling about his music that he should have had. I think he had the J. D. Short idea — he put the other guy way up above himself and he didn't like that. He done it himself, they didn't set themselves up there. I got along all right with him, but he was a difficult guy to get along with all right.

I can't pin it down, but I also met Washboard Sam at one of these sessions for Bluebird. We met at the studio and I done some sounds with him, but not recording.[25] I also met Robert Nighthawk about the same time I met Sonny Boy. Robert was playing down on Thirteenth and Biddle — that's where I got acquainted with him. Robert was a good hustler: he'd go make him a job.

Nighthawk was into a lot of entertaining-style music, dance music, and what have you. Because you sure couldn't dance off his blues — boy, they were as draggiest as they get! And in most cases Robert kept some gal with him, and whoever she was, he put her to work. She's gonna do something. He carried them to school and put them to work and most of them qualified for him. He got them going and he carried them in the studio with him. Ann Sortier worked with him in Chicago for a long time. They were pretty famous on the South Side. Nighthawk traveled a lot; he was in St. Louis and in Mississippi. He made a song about the Brickyard. I know where it is — I've been there — it's little area of Clarksdale, Mississippi.[26]

Nighthawk had ways more like Robert Johnson than anybody else that I know. Quiet conversation — you'd have to bring it out of him — just a quiet kind of guy. But he done some real nice stuff there on his slide. I think Tampa Red was his idol. He done lot of Tampa Red's everything — vocals towards Tampa and of course his guitar was directed at Tampa's style.

Nighthawk was instrumental in Muddy Waters getting into it, I do know that. He'd talk about it, about the guy he was training to play slide. He referred to it quite often. When I first knew Nighthawk, I was beginning to be bold on the piano. I'd be telling him about what Roosevelt showed me, and he'd tell me about what he showed Muddy Waters.

Last time I really saw Nighthawk was in Chicago — it must have been around Forty-seventh Street. He was playing there, him and this gal, and boy, he was breakin' 'em down. He kept that house packed. That's the last time I saw Robert. It was soon after Sonny Boy Williamson died.

Joe Willie Wilkins teamed up with Roosevelt Sykes when Roosevelt was in Memphis — Joe lived there in Memphis. Roosevelt and Joe worked around and through the country and eventually wound up in St. Louis. I was working down at Fourteenth and Cass at a place called Joe's Corner, but I gave the job to Roosevelt and Joe Willie, and that's when they started staying with me. Joe Willie was younger than me — at the time he was somewhere just past a kid. They also played up on North Market and Spring; the building is still there — I think it's a church or something. Joe played with Roosevelt quite a bit, probably more than a year, just the two of them.

To pinpoint where Roosevelt Sykes was at any given time would be almost impossible. He was worse than Big Joe Williams. Big Joe would travel the States over — at any minute he could be gone — and Roosevelt was just about as bad. Roosevelt traveled all over — Chicago, Memphis, Detroit — but he'd wind up right back in St. Louis. St. Louis was more or less a foundation for him, and he depended on me a lot. If things got a little rough for him, he'd come back to see what Mule was doing. St. Louis was his headquarters until he suddenly went to New Orleans, and he stayed there longer than I'd ever known him to stay in one place.

During the 1940s was the first time Roosevelt and I were in the South together, and we were just freelancing. We were working at a place called Tobacco George's on Triggs and Florida in Memphis. This one day we had got paid off, and Roosevelt went and bought him a new straw hat. Anyway, we were coming away from the club and we walked over to Horn Lake Road, and two detectives drove up and jumped out and questioned us. We were answering questions, and one of them just out of spite reached up on Roosevelt's head and snatched his hat off. "Nigger, you got this hat. Where in the hell did you get a pretty hat like this?" And he threw it down and stomped on it.

Roosevelt looked at me and I looked at him and he gave me a sign. I said no. Roosevelt stood there and looked at the man and tears come out of his eyes. And the man told him, "Nigger, you wanna be smart?" Roosevelt didn't say nothing. So the other man said, "Come on, let the man alone."

You know, that was a time. It hurt so bad until it hurts now, really it does. That was so uncalled for, so out of bounds. That fellow got his kicks out of doing that. But it wasn't the way he thought, really it wasn't. Because if I hadn't given Roosevelt the "No" sign he wouldn't have lived — so help me God, he would have been dead, one of them would have been dead.

Roosevelt wasn't no pushover now, he sure wasn't. I don't know if he could have shot Roosevelt or not, because he was standing too close to Roosevelt and he may not have been able to get to that gun. If Roosevelt had've went for him, the other one would have to kill me, because I was going for him. There would have been two people dead, me and Roosevelt, or two officers dead. And for what? Nothing. And if we'd killed them, that would have been four people dead, because they'd have killed us later on.

Our luck was really down on us right about then. Roosevelt was playing for little or nothing, and I was just tagging along. We went to Helena, Arkansas, and damn if we didn't get arrested over there. Somebody over there called in on Roosevelt for doing something, and they come by and arrested him and me and carried us to jail.

Now Roosevelt's brother Rufus was also in jail down there, but he was driving for the sheriff — the man that run everything. Rufus was supposed to be a prisoner. Now we're in jail and Rufus hears about it and he tells the sheriff to go and turn his brother out — he ain't stole nothing. And that's what he done. He called down there and told them to turn us loose.

When Rufus got off work, he'd come by where we were staying, and he was driving the city or the state car and carrying a .45 and nobody was with him! There's a lot of people that understand it and know how it is down there, and there's people that would think that's not true. This is true. Rufus worked for the sheriff around the house, in the yard: he kept the car clean and drove him where he wanted to go. Now if he was going to be riding along with the sheriff, he should carry a gun. What he actually turned out to be was a deputy sheriff serving time! Oh boy!

But that was the system, and I'm glad of it, because that's what saved us. They would probably have had us framed, and the first thing you know, we would probably have went to one of them farms down there. They had it waiting on us.

Finally, Rufus told the sheriff he wanted to leave town. The sheriff told him okay and took his gun back and all that and told him, if he ever want to come back down there, you know where I'm at. Rufus left there and come to St. Louis and jumped out a window to keep from getting arrested in a crap game. He broke his leg and he had to go back down there to survive, because by this time Roosevelt had left St. Louis and went to Chicago.

While I was down in Helena one time, I met Red Eyed Jesse Bell. He also played piano, but I never did actually get to hear him play. Roosevelt always referred to him; he'd play a number and he'd always refer to it as "Red Eyed Jesse Bell played this." It was a very peculiar number — I tried to learn it, but I never did get it together, so I never did fool with it much after that. But it was different, like "44 Blues." Roosevelt's "44" are different from anything you hear anybody play. And so was this Jesse Bell number.[27] I think Roosevelt got "West Helena Blues" from Jesse Bell, either him or his baby brother Walter Sykes. Walter had two famed numbers that he could beat Roosevelt with, and they were "44" and "Roll and Tumble." He could really play them. "Roll and Tumble" is played on piano. I don't do it all that well, but when I was working hard I was doing it much better than I'm doing it now. Walter Sykes was a genius at those songs, and this is one of the things that caused Roosevelt and I to get together. He got a little jealous of his brothers, Jesse and Walter, and he kind of hired me away from them.

Roosevelt and I traveled from St. Louis all the way to the Gulf Coast, New Orleans, and all the states in between, just hoboing. Driving didn't come into my category then. The first car I had was a T Model Ford and then an A Model Ford. And this was the car Walter Davis, Big Joe, Sonny Boy, and I were in when we all went up to Aurora to record.

The time Roosevelt and I played in Memphis was when we met Speckled Red — he was kinda all around. I remember him distinctly playing that number that he made so famous, "Dirty Dozens."[28] When Red lived in St. Louis, he used to hang around on Enright and Taylor at the filling station. He used to hang around there daily long before he died.[29]

Roosevelt had been in Indianapolis during the time St. Louis Jimmy lived there — they were pretty tight buddies. Then Roosevelt moved back to Chicago before these breaks come to him, and that's when he took to the road. He had a full-size band, two or three brass, and for a period of time two guitars, a drummer, and himself. This was the smallest size band he had; sometimes, depending on the kind of job, he would pick up guys on a one- or two-time deal. A guy in Indianapolis was booking him; he furnished them with the bus and all this stuff.

I was living at 2320 Carr Street when he first hit the road, and if he had any spare time he'd put up there with me, him and his band boys. I could save them a whole lot of money. Sometimes they'd be trying to beat the hotel thing, and sleeping on that bus can get to be old. Later on I started joining up with them — this was when he was at his peak — and that's when I kinda got burned out with traveling around.

There was a fellow that used to drive Roosevelt around that we called Humble Servant — Emmett Hill was his name. He also used to bring in Memphis Slim and Guitar Murphy and book them around. But Humble Servant was a Minnesota Fats when he was traveling with Roosevelt. He was a great pool hustler. And it wasn't no expense to Roosevelt at all; in fact it was an asset to him, because if he hit those towns he could make as much money as Roosevelt right quick. Then he would drive the car or whatever.

Humble Servant eventually went into gospel quartets and things, and when he died he had a church over on Chouteau, and they went to calling him Reverend Hill. He'd laugh about it — he'd say he wasn't no reverend. But he loved quartet singing and quit his hustling. Guitar Murphy used to play for his gospel groups. Murphy was around here quite a bit.[30]

But Roosevelt Sykes was the most outstanding piano player in the city of St. Louis. Henry Brown was really recognized, and Pinetop picked up quite a bit from Roosevelt, but Sykes was *it* in the blues field.

"A VERY GOOD HUSTLE"

My friend Harvey McAllister and I got inducted into the service together, and we were sent down to Greensboro, North Carolina, for training. We got together as a team and we were both pretty smooth in making a living in what we know to do. He was the gambler, and I assisted him because I could write and he could read. When I say that, marking cards is what I'm basically talking about. I knew all the details and could do it about as fast as anybody I know, and he could read everything that I marked.

When we went in the service, we picked up quite a bit of money right fast. But one of the sergeants hollered wolf on us, and they had an investigation. We'd beat him out of his money, and they took the cards because the guy was hollering that they was marked. They took those cards and put them under a microscope and examined them, and they couldn't find nothing. But I'm standing as far as I am to you looking right at it and those guys couldn't find it. They dismissed the case. The army wouldn't like to hear that.

However, it did throw me off guard a little bit. If it would have happened again with a different person, they would have had to say there was something to it. We would have been in a lot of trouble, and to the stockade we would have been gone. But quite a bit of money had been passed our way before we got squawked on, so we kinda lightened up on that. We went back down to the craps.

But what we'd do with the cards was this. We found out the popular cards they'd play with, we'd go into the town to one of those small drugstores and buy them all out. We'd write on them, pack them up, and take them back to the drugstore. They didn't give you your money back, but they are just back in the store. Now they didn't play with no raggedy decks, they kept fresh decks. So this was right down our alley. Now if they get superstitious about our cards, go and buy a new deck! So they go and buy a new deck — we ain't touched them, so they think. But we have.

Then all of a sudden I got discharged. Well, the truth is, I didn't feel that I should soldier. I didn't feel that I had nobody that I was mad at. This lieutenant was gonna tell me what I should do — my enemy and all of that. I was kinda refusing to do things then. So he wanted to talk to me man to man. He said, "That's your enemy."

I stopped him right there. I said, "How do I know that?"

He said, "Because they are the enemy of the United States."

I said, "Well, that's not my enemy, that's the enemy to the country where I live. If I was going to fight my enemy, do you know who it would be?"

He said, "No."

I said, "You! I got people back there in St. Louis right now, and there's places they can't go and eat. There's places right here off camp and in the camp that I'm not allowed there. So if I was gonna fight my enemy, it would be you."

That changed his attitude towards me. He looked at me a while and said, "Why do you say that, soldier?"

I said, "Just like I told you, all these things that I feel I'm entitled to, I'm being deprived of. I don't see no need for you or your people to deprive me of them."

So right then I earned me a way to a vacant barracks with nobody in it but me — that's what I earned from that conversation. The lieutenant couldn't be that dumb — he was smart enough to know that if I got into conversation with other soldiers, I might poison their minds. So right away they got me away from these people, because this rotten apple's gonna mess the barrel up, and they didn't want that. I wasn't ordered away from the other men, but I was never called to duties, therefore that eliminated me from being in conversation with others.

This is gonna sound a little awkward, but believe it or not, I predicted the length of my stay in the army. I wasn't a psychic and don't claim to be, but I sure named when I would get back home. I said the limit would be three months, and that's all the time I served, three months. Just long enough to become a soldier — they couldn't take that away from me.

Anyway, I was discharged. They had a pretty name for it: C.D.D. That's "Can't Do Duties." It really means a medical discharge — it had to be converted into a medical discharge — it's double-talk stuff. If you can't do duties, you're sick; if you're well, you could do duties. And today they won't go with me on that. They said I was physically unfit.

Now what happened was, I did lose a lot of weight. I also learnt to do something to defeat the doctors: I psyched myself into controlling my heartbeat. It's deep concentration, and I could control it, and it baffled them doctors like mad. But I regretted it later on, because the thing kinda got out of hand with me after I got out of the service. Somehow I would spark it and it would reoccur, and it took me a long time to dismiss that. That worried me for a while, but I finally come out of it. I wouldn't want to do that no more. But the record shows that the condition was caused by the service. Maybe it was, but I helped it.

I don't know if it's really fair to say that I lived in Chicago, because I was always coming back to St. Louis, but I was calling Chicago the place where I lived at that time. At the time my first wife and I had just busted down, so I didn't have a family. I was in and out of Chicago periodically from 1945 almost up into the 1950s.

I just went up there to be visiting and didn't leave, so I just stayed around there. The first thing I did was to find out where Roosevelt was playing at. Him and Lonnie Johnson was playing at Thirtieth and Indiana, so I made it there. And that's where I started back on my music sounds.

I was staying at Thirty-first and Giles, and this boy had a little weekend thing going there at the house. They'd have little games going there on the weekend. If push come to shove I could gamble — and I would too, because I knew how — but I never did do it as I had before. But things got a little rough a couple of times, so I eased in the game and pulled me a stake out. But I never did want to gamble; if I knew I could get rich I still wouldn't do it.

At first I didn't know exactly where Sonny Boy Williamson was, but he heard about me being in town. He was living on South Parkway then, and he found me, and we started bumming around together. I was also living around the corner from Bowtie — Eddie Boyd — and I got acquainted with him. Otha Brown lived not too far from me.[1] I lived at 3112 Giles and Otha lived right there on Thirty-first Street. And so did Curtis Jones. Curtis was a unique piano player, but I never did play with him.

Jew Town was Sonny Boy's hangout, over on the West Side.[2] We used to have music duels, Otha Brown and Little Walter, Eddie El, Sonny Boy, and myself.[3] We used to all get together and do what they call battle royals. I would work with Sonny Boy, and Otha would work with Little Walter. Eddie was working with another fellow, his name was Pinkie something.

We'd get on the street corners and it was a very good hustle. Sometimes I would have a little advantage because I'd have Eddie El with me. Then we would all just get together and jam it on out. We'd be on the same corner and we'd switch off: they'd do a session, we'd do a session. But it was some good music — it was really beautiful, and it was a booster to all of us. We all learned a lot from this kind of experience. It was very entertaining, and we would pick up coins on them corners.

We'd get to doing a battle royal and the street would get blocked; sooner or later the police would come by and tell us to scatter. We actually wasn't doing anything but blocking traffic; because so many people had gathered around, cars couldn't get by. But we made money with that. Eddie El and I would also go on South Parkway and find ourselves a vacant bench and get together with those two guitars and pick ourselves up some change. When you picked up ten or fifteen dollars, that wasn't bad.

Now this was also a scam to put you in any of them clubs you wanted to be in. See, news gets around, and them club owners would come out there and see these guys who got on a corner like this. You could be beneficial to his place, so you'd get a job right away. I got a lot of experience out of that kind of a thing. But I always did know that I didn't have to worry about being hungry nowhere — that was in my hand and on my instrument. That was a meal ticket at any time, and I knew that. Now I wasn't too sure if it would put me in a bed and put me to sleep, but I knew it was a meal ticket.

I never did join up with any particular bands to work with or ask any of them to work with me; I was kind of a soloist. The truth is, at that time most of us were single acts. Roosevelt was a single act — occasionally St. Louis Jimmy would come by and do some vocals with him. Sunnyland Slim was a single act. Eddie El was totally a single act and so was Eddie Boyd until his recording came up.[4] Nobody was concerned about nobody; everybody was doing their own thing and getting away with it. Bumble Bee Slim, everybody was more or less single acts. Bumble Bee Slim had a pretty good following.[5] I saw him somewhere on the extreme South Side — he was entertaining pretty much around them clubs there. What he played was pretty much expected, but he was kinda limited on his guitar playing. I also ran across Kokomo Arnold somewhere at some of those night spots.[6]

I also met Doctor Clayton there in Chicago on the street and at the place where he was playing. We'd eat at a little old restaurant there on Thirty-first Street — it was more or less a chili joint. For the little bit I associated with Doctor Clayton, all I could say about him was he was just an ordinary person, just another person. But he wasn't no great dresser. He didn't worry too much about that. I've heard Robert Jr. Lockwood say that he'd worked with Doctor Clayton. Robert was pretty wide range there in Chicago. Robert was and still is a good blending person with sounds — he can blend with anything just about, and it don't have to be the blues pattern either, he's just good. Truth is, he amazed me down there in Louisiana when we were together at the World's Fair. I knew he played, but I didn't know he was as good as he was in jazz. He's heavy with that stuff.[7]

I never did meet Cripple Clarence Lofton, but I heard about him all the time. Every time I was in Chicago, Sonny Boy would be talking about him — he was Sonny Boy's head support man. Sonny Boy was by him almost like Walter Davis was by me; they stayed together pretty tight. But Roosevelt Sykes was the most popular guy around there at that time because he was more or less fresh in Chicago, he wasn't burnt out. Lonnie Johnson was burnt out, he'd been there — you know how that goes. Sonny Boy was real, real famous but he was burned some, because he'd been there quite a spell before I went there. Sonny Boy would travel back home to wherever. He would go back to where Lacy Belle was and then back to Chicago if she wouldn't come with him. I also saw Memphis Slim there — he was playing out at the Flamingo Inn or something on Roosevelt Road. I'd met Slim before in St. Louis. I went back out there another time and he asked me to come and work with him, but I didn't go. Guitar Murphy wasn't with him then. I didn't see Slim again until we met at the Chicago Blues Festival in 1986.

I never met Muddy Waters then. Muddy and I really got acquainted in East St. Louis. When we first met I knew him, but he didn't know me. Gabriel the disk jockey gave a thing at the Majestic Theater in East St. Louis, and Muddy Waters and myself were booked over there.[8] But I met the famous people in Chicago. I met Tampa Red and Big Bill Broonzy. Big Bill and Sonny Boy were a pretty good team for a while. But after a while I just said to myself that I was tired of Chicago and I came back out of there.

Anyway, back in St. Louis I met up with another girl named Teenie Mae Patterson. I ran into her in the street or a tavern or something like that. I think I took up with her out of sympathy because she had two boys with no help, no support, and she was really trying to find ways to feed the kids. So I met her a couple of times at the same spot, and we finally got together. At this particular time I was driving a cab. I drove a cab off and on for years, not constantly, because I'd be away doing other things. I worked for the Blue Jay Central Cab for a long time and also Checker Cab for a little while. I drove cabs even before I worked at the Grand Central Hotel.

I stayed with her pretty good; 1955 is when she and I separated. That stayed common-law. She turned out to be that person again. She didn't want to leave me, but she got a little out of line with her carrying on, and I didn't want to go with this kind of a thing.

But what happened: I had bought an old car and I would let her use it going back and forth. She was working downtown cleaning offices and whatnot. When she didn't use the car, she got her special boyfriend to ride. That wasn't so much of a problem of mine. I knew things wasn't what they ought to be, but I didn't let that bother me too much. But she had a little money then, and she done got out there and got wild. I even got her a job at the Albany Hotel at Page and Euclid. She was managing the hotel, and that gave her a little more money. The Albany was also the last place Walter Davis worked at before he died.

So she's getting unruly and she don't want to do nothing I say now. She thinks she can handle me any kind of way because I'm so soft. So I decided no, we won't let it go this way. But before I cut loose from her, this guy had sent around to the house for her, and that kinda burned me, you know. This guy got his nerve! So when she came in I said, "You gonna pay your boyfriend a visit?" She said, "No, I ain't." I said, "Yes, you are." So I insisted in her going up there. I didn't go there to do any damages, I went up there to talk to him, to find out a little bit more about what was happening. I got up there and he wanted to get all funny, so then I had to chastise him. I went prepared if I had to, because by this time I was working at the Grand Central Hotel and I kept a .38 strapped on me at all time.

So this guy got a little out of turn and wanted to do something about it. I told him, "Don't do that," but he insisted in making the effort to do it. I didn't shoot him, but I slapped him upside the head a couple of times with the pistol. Then I brought her on down and explained to her that we was no longer: "You're on your own." She eventually moved to California.

The Grand Central Hotel was right on the corner of Jefferson and Pine. I ran that place for a long time. Those hotel days were really interesting. It wasn't black owned but it was a typical black hotel. It was *the* black hotel of the city. It wasn't the only one, but it was the most renowned. Every famous black person lived there. If you came to St. Louis and didn't stay in the Grand Central, you hadn't been to St. Louis. In later years blacks started going to the Booker Washington Hotel, which was on Kingshighway, and it began to equal the Grand Central. The Calumet Hotel was on Jefferson and Locust, and Walter Davis managed that. Then later on, Walter handled the Albany Hotel on Page. I started out with Walter at the Calumet Hotel, then I went to the Grand Central.

There's a lot of money in this business if you run it right and the company gets what is rightfully theirs. That's all this man wanted, what was rightfully his. He would tell us, "Give me my money and don't let me catch you doing nothing wrong." Well, that was the story there. He got his money from each clerk that was there — the other person would see to that. If he didn't know how to handle himself, that was his tough luck, and we wouldn't teach nobody.

I could make three hundred to four hundred dollars on a weekend, and through the week I could take all my expenses, but I wouldn't get greedy. But do you know what my paycheck was? Thirty-five dollars, that's all it was. Time and time again he'd say, "I'm not gonna pay you nothing because you're gonna make way more than I'm gonna pay you." He knew exactly what was happening.

He put in about 35 or 40 rooms a night for transients, and they would get used up. Weekends, that wasn't even a starter; I could have used 150 rooms on a weekend, but he wouldn't put over 50 or 60 rooms in on the weekend. Now, being transient, I'd use every room the maid made up, cash on the register. Then they kept coming in, and I'd repeat that. I'd put on new linen and start using the same rooms over again. Now this is the trick part about it: I had to keep another register in case something went wrong, then I could handle it. I would go through the same room setup, and the second time around, it's mine. And sometimes the third time around, and that would be mine. But I got him his money and that's what he expected, and he was satisfied with that.

I had several bellboys. Some of them wasn't no good, but when I got me a good bellboy, I took care of him. If he made me five rooms, he had him five dollars. If he made me twenty rooms, he had twenty dollars that night — or better. And the people that wanted bellboy service, that was all his. If he went out and made any connections, then that was money for him. The bellboys were driving expensive cars. Walter Davis was also making real heavy money, real heavy money.

It was a good job, it was a soft job, but there was danger there. There was the danger of being held up or the wrong thing going on. Maybe some man catches his woman in there and wants to do something about it and you say something and get killed. There's a lot of dangers that can lurk around one of those jobs.

I had some problems, but I thought I knew how to handle it, and I'm pretty sure I did, because nothing drastic ever came out of it. I always tried to maintain cool — I tried to stay cool so I could think clear. I would never rush into nothing, and I think that had a lot to do with me surviving in a lot of ways.

One time a guy came in there and he was supposed to be the boss of that part of town — you know you run into that. His name was Cleveland, and when I started to work there, he checked me out to see if I was soft. So when I found out he was checking me out I just told him in a polite way, "Cleveland, now I'm in charge here. I'd appreciate it if you would abide by the regulations of the hotel, and I'm sure we'll get along." I'm sounding real good to him now, because he's sure he can run this thing. This little soft so-and-so, female-minded man — I'll put it that way.

So later on he came back with a couple of girls, and one of them said something and he started with her in the hotel. I said, "Cleveland, you don't know me and I don't know you, and I've asked you not to do all these kind of things." Oh man, he went to blowin'. He started towards me. I said, "No, don't come this way. I'm not approaching you, and don't you approach me. If you want to start that, the best thing you can do is dismiss yourself from the hotel."

Well, he wouldn't take that. My voice didn't sound harsh enough for him — he thought I should be hollerin' and crying by that time. So when he started up there, I just knocked that automatic out and said, "You want to go out the door, Cleveland?"

He said, "Man, you can't put me outta here!" Pow! I shot right in the floor over by him.

"Man, I'll get outta here!"

I said, "No, you don't want to get out. Don't get out now, wait 'til I get there." I got over there and rapped him upside the head with the automatic and said, "Now you go, and don't come back."

That cleared it up. The news got around: that little black nigger so-and-so in there is a mean son of a bitch. It hurt my business for a while, but it cleared it up. From then on I was respected, and nobody come in running over me and I didn't have to get loud with nobody for years to come. But I had to build a quick reputation; if you don't, them people will run you out of them places. Because sooner or later somebody would have come in there and either get me, or I would have had to get them. See, I started at the top; he bossed that neighborhood for a few years.

About a few weeks later Cleveland sent me word, asking me could he come back in and apologize for how he had acted. I told him if he was gonna obey the hotel rules and regulations, to come back in like everybody else. It worked out all right — he finally rated me as a nice guy. But most of the people around in the neighborhood was ready to whoop him, because what they thought he was, he wasn't. Some terrible things happened — that's what human nature's about.

We had a lot of things going for us in the hotel business. Keeping your nose clean was one of the major things. You couldn't involve yourself with some of the activities that would be going on around the hotel — stay clear of that. I don't care how great the hotel is, there's always gonna be that certain something that can come in there and connect you with bad things if you're not careful. The law in St. Louis at that particular time was real prejudice towards black business, hotels, or what have you, if they looked like they were successful. Like dope and the thugs: you don't want to associate yourself with them. If you wish, you could rent them a room, but you had to be careful with them, because they would plant stuff around if you wasn't watching. And when the big thing come off, they would point the finger right at you. There's tricks in every game you go into.

The place I was working at was bad about that. I got a good education out of it, because the content of the hotel was exactly what we're talking about: nothing but prostitutes and dope pushers and all of this kind of a thing. The truth is, I had to be a little bit on the side that I didn't want to be on in order to remain there. I would buckle that automatic around my waist and that's how I had to carry myself around there at all times.

We had terrific transient trade — when I went there this is what it was. It was a great transit hotel and it was an addict hotel — when I say "addict" I mean dope users. They are the people that you can make a lot of money off of because they are not going to get tired and stay at home. These people are gonna be on that job because they got to have that money — their addiction says come there.

Those gals — nice-looking gals — they'd get out there on the street and they would solicit. There was one girl there and she looked to be a kid. I think she was about twenty-seven or twenty-eight years old, but she looked like a teenager, and her name was Nina, and she would make forty or fifty dollars a night, easy.

I got an education from a lot of things there, the unusual type people that come in there. You would think they were headed toward the room for sex, but not always so. There were two guys that used to come in there that I know about, but one specifically. He would come in there and ask about this little girl, Nina. And when the bellboy brought her forward, he would stand in conversation with her for about three or four minutes and that was it. He done that a couple of times. The next time he called back for her, I said I want to see this one out. I was sitting behind the desk and I told Nina to come up front and talk to him where I could see them, and she did. And that's where I learned my lesson at — the guy's kick was coming in.

So then I pulled the bellboy's coat. When he came in again and asked for Nina, I told the bellboy to tell him that Nina wouldn't come unless you give her some kind of money. The bellboy told him, you have to give at least twenty dollars. He gave him the twenty dollars, and she came up and talked with him, and that was it. That's twenty dollars he done wasted. Of course after the game got to going, naturally we ran him away — we hit him too hard, he couldn't stand the pressure. He had to go find him another spot to go talk at.

A few thing happened while I was down there. One prostitute went in the room with this guy, and she was found dead. She wasn't strangled — autopsy didn't find nothing but the sex part of it. About a few months later some other girl was with this fellow in a car somewhere parked behind a coal shed, and she was dead. Nothing about the body demolished — I guess sex stopped the heart or something. Later on they found another woman dead in a hotel up on Franklin Avenue and traced it back to the same man as having sex with them.

Anyway, about six months or a year later, he came into the West End Hotel, and I happened to be there.[9] Now I don't know who he is or nothing, but I'd seen him come into my hotel down there a time or two. I was on the evening shift, and he sent for the bellboy to bring him up something to drink, and he asked me would I come up and drink some with him; of course, I refused. I didn't notice when I rented him the room how depressed the man was. Anyway, that night he put a sheet around the closet and tied it, got up on the chair, and hung himself. The maid found him next shift. Anyway, they come to the conclusion that all of this was because of the deaths that he caused.

I also run into some pretty tough things at the Grand Central from the police department. This notorious fellow — a black policeman called Fred Grimes — he done some things that were unacceptable. He used his own black people for his promotion. When I say "used," I mean used. And not the wrongdoers — he used anybody he could to get promoted. When he died, his wife said she didn't want no parts of it — do anything you want with the body. You didn't hear too many good things about him.

Fred Grimes wanted me to help him bust some of the people in the hotel, and I wouldn't do that. He had been in several times before and tried to order me around. I told him, "No, you have to take that up with the company boss. I've got a job here and I'm only doing my job."

So this time he come in with a sawed-off shotgun and he was waving it around and he told me to give him the keys. I said, "No, I can't do that. The keys are hanging there. Now I can't stop you from getting them, but I'm not going to give them to you." And he started to waving his gun over there at me. I told him, "Now look, I'm not licensed to carry no gun out of here, but I've got a gun on me — I want you to know that. Now if you don't intend to do something to me with your gun, point it the other way."

So he pointed it the other way and told me to give him the keys again. I said, "I'll come from behind the counter and you can come on back here and get the keys." But he wouldn't go on back and get them. If I would have gave him the keys, it would have been the clerk giving him the authority to go in, but I wouldn't do it. He didn't want to deal with the company, so he was trying to fool me.

So he called me a few names and talked about me, and I smiled at him. He turned around and went back out. He waited outside, and I think he busted a couple of the girls when they came out, but that wasn't what he wanted. He might have had a lead on some dope — I don't know — but I couldn't aid him in that. If he'd brought a warrant, he'd have had to have had something to bring the warrant for. Toting a warrant around in your pocket and ain't got no arrest to make, that's no good. Fred Grimes was a kinda overbearing officer, but like everybody else, when he found out he didn't have people to run over, he kinda ceased to be the mean man he was. I refused to let him just push me around, although I tried to stay within the bounds of the law.

But you can't even imagine now what that area around the hotel was like then. It was jumping. Jefferson and all that neighborhood was it. One of the classic restaurants for blacks was there; Jesse Johnson opened up the DeLuxe Cafe right around the corner off Market Street, on Jefferson between Market and Chestnut. And the railroads were operating — Union Station attracted a lot of people, and the Pullman Porters and all of them would come to the hotel.

seven

"MAKING IT PRETTY DON'T HELP A BIT"

In the early 1950s I put together a band, and we stayed together for a long time. I had Roosevelt Carmichael on piano; Henry — I forgot his last name, but he was my drummer; and the man on saxophone had worked with Walter Davis and I, his name was Johnny Moore, he was on the "Tears Come Rollin' Down" session. And I had three girls; they done dancing and this kind of a thing and one of them was a vocalist. One girl, her name was Blue but we call her Cookie, and she was Miss Callie's niece, the lady who used to have the place over on Delmar. And there was another girl who used to call herself the Countess, and they would do a special in my show. I had a pretty healthy setup; those girls kept the show pretty much alive.

We worked at this little old theater down in the city. It was a movie show, and they used to have vaudeville shows with the movies. I worked at the West End Waiters[1] and the Glass Bar[2] and there were quite a few more places out in the country. We played all over, all kinds of places. I was doing whatever was necessary then, even a little jazz. We weren't calling ourselves anything, I was just using my name.

The first gig that I made that was successful was in Clayton.[3] And at that time Clayton was pretty well open — the place where blacks shouldn't be. It was pretty rough out there, but being musicians we didn't have no problems. We were accepted out there, and I worked a few places out there.

From then on I was just warm all the way through and I got hotter
and hotter. I was catering to dance music and everything then, and with
the band I could produce dance music. I was a crowd drawer and I
could also play with the rhythm for the dance thing like B. B. King
does. See, if B. B. King had to play for a dance he couldn't play for it
either, but with a band he can. The same thing with me — I can play
all the dance stuff necessary.

Johnny Moore would have his saxophone in his hand and a gun-
nysack on a stick on his back when he went on a gig, and in that sack
were his drinks. It could be anywhere from a quart to a half-gallon to
a gallon of wine. You could see him daily — he'd have a pretty good
size bottle. He didn't want people to know how much he consumed
of that stuff — this way he could be private with his own thing. Johnny
eventually left St. Louis and moved to California, and I heard a rumor that he drank himself to death. I could see it easily. He played
with my band for a long time, and that's how I come to hook him up
with Walter Davis and I.

We played quite a few places until I got sick, and when that happened I cooled it down — it didn't go no further. And I decided I
wouldn't try and go back into it right away. Henry the drummer, he
got ill and he passed on, Johnny left for California, and Roosevelt
Carmichael started working with James Deshay — he played with
James Deshay until he died. He was an extremely good piano player
too. He had his own style and he could do Roosevelt Sykes — he could
imitate just about all of them — but I liked his own style the best; he
was better with his own thing.

Another time I put a band together, and the musicians all tried to
carry me to school. They want to start telling me about the different
notes and all of that. I told them I don't read, I just make sounds that
correspond with one another. And they said, "Well, you have to go back
to school before we can do this and that." I said, "Well then, it's you
all that don't qualify for me, not me that don't qualify for you." As
Roosevelt Sykes always said, and I use the term: "Now if you all that
great, don't expect me to work with you. You're great enough, you
should be able to work with me!" Anyway, it didn't soak in none, so it
wasn't too long, maybe a month, that I handled them.

But I didn't play much at that time, and I was almost out of it except for some things I wanted to do private. I think one or two times Joe Willie Wilkins or Roosevelt Sykes came through St. Louis, and I would pick up the guitar and go over a few things. At one time I had Joe Willie Wilkins, Roosevelt Sykes, his wife and daughter, and Rice Miller all staying with me.

Joe Willie and I were real pals. I went to his house in Memphis to visit him. Joe Willie and I got to be almost as close as Roosevelt and I was. I met Son House when he was down there in Memphis with Joe Willie Wilkins. This was back in the 1960s, quite a while before Joe Willie died.[4]

When Joe Willie would come in town, I'd give him a room at the hotel, where he could be where I was at. We'd jam on the guitars and things, stay down there, and put stuff together. I got one number that I do the music sound, one part come from Clifford Gibson, and I developed the music from Joe Willie: "Tired of Being Mistreated."[5] It's Clifford Gibson's title, but the music style is totally different. This come from a little thing Joe Willie and I cooked up at the hotel, little simple thing. Gabriel was crazy about that number. Boy, just before they kicked him out at KATZ he would play that number three or four times a night.

I played with Rice Miller a few times around here in the city of St. Louis, and he actually lived with me for a while. I don't know the history on Rice Miller, but he was older than John Lee Williamson, but John Lee made the first fame on the harmonica.[6] Rice Miller tagged himself because of Sonny Boy Williamson's fame. Then the original Sonny Boy got credit for working for the "King Biscuit Time," which he didn't.

I heard the story of John Lee going down to Helena, Arkansas, to try and stop Rice Miller using the name, but I wouldn't want to verify that. I never heard John Lee say that he had done a thing like that, but he was aware that this man Rice Miller was doing it. I guess Rice Miller's intention was to make the people think that he was the real Sonny Boy, and it did get him a lot of recognition. Nobody can know unless you research with King Biscuit whether they thought he was the original at first. I'm sure they knew about it before it was over with.

But as long as he was doing a good job, what difference did it make? But he made his fame by the way he blew his harp and not because his name was there. He used the name to open the door, but when he got in there, he done his thing.

I guess it could sound like a brag thing, but I was pretty well always on solid ground. And Roosevelt, Sonny Boy, and all the rest of them guys would have certain times when they would run into the low end of things — they were kinda floaters. So if they were down in luck in the city, I would scout up some jobs and put them up until they could get a foothold. I used to do that with a lot music people coming through.

Somewhere in this time was when I met Albert King.[7] Roosevelt Sykes, Rice Miller, and I were playing at a little tavern on Nineteenth and Delmar, and Albert King had come to shoot me down, as we used to call it. It was the first time him and I had a battle royal. He'd heard me play but he really hadn't heard me stretch out.

So I gave him the bandstand and he played. He had that peculiar style which sounds damn good, really. He worked out and the crowd accepted it pretty good. When I got back on the stage, I said to my-self, "I've got to bear down a little bit and try and compensate some. I got the job and guy's gonna come in and influence the crowd better than me!"

So Roosevelt got on the piano and played, then I called his attention to playing one of the numbers where I take over, "I've Got Tired of Your Lowdown Dirty Ways," one of Leroy Carr's numbers, which I had rearranged. So I think we ran neck and neck there, kind of com-promised the thing out. And that's the first time Albert had ever talked to me. He said, "Man, you know I'm gonna have to give it to you. I didn't think that was in you at all."

I said, "Well, thank you. I don't always do my best."

He said, "I know, because I've heard you play a couple of times and to me you must have been just laying back." I don't push too hard all the time. We had fun with that one.

Then Rice Miller got on his harmonica. There was somebody else there — I can't think of who that person was — but they thought they could blow harmonica, and they were trying to work with Rice Miller, but he was a little tough to work with. I can't exactly describe the kind of person he was, but if you didn't work with him to his satisfaction, you didn't work with him at all. That was to be known, no matter where you was. It make no difference how many people were there, he'd just tell you, "Man, you're in my way. There ain't nothing you can do for me."

Rice Miller would drink, and I could say some of his ways could be contributed to his drinking. He would drink and he would get pretty tilted. You can always say drinking has some influence over you, otherwise you wouldn't follow through with it. As much as I know about drinking, which is as much as anybody, when you respond to what alcohol does for you, you can't remain normal, because every drink is gonna call for that other one.

I don't think anyone drank any more than Henry Townsend and Roosevelt Sykes. And by the same token I don't think anybody ever drank less than my other associate, Walter Davis. If he drank a half-pint in his whole lifetime, that's more than I know him to drink. He'd say, "Give me a shot." He'd get him a whiskey glass and just cover the bottom of the glass and throw it up. And it was effective to him, that two or three drops. A teaspoonful was it for him. Now you wouldn't get him to do that no more in two years — he just wasn't designed to fool with it. Roosevelt and I was just like fishes, but we never went to the extreme. Like now if I drink, I'll get a little loud in conversation but I'll be rational. I won't get so I won't know what I'm saying or droopy lipped, and I've maintained that all my life.

✳ ✳ ✳

In the late 1950s I married a woman named Nina, and that lasted about five years, up to about 1964. Pete Bogans married us; he was a minister at the time. I was working at the Independent Merchants on Grand Avenue in sales and collection, and we were living in the projects down on Twelfth Street.

When we separated I wasn't gonna stay down there, but I didn't have nowhere to put the furniture because I didn't have no house. She thought that she could move in with her uncles on Euclid Avenue, so

I told her to take the furniture and we would come to some sort of agreement later on, because I would want a bed or something when I got ready to get a place.

So when I found a place I called her and told her I'd like to pick up some of the stuff, and she said okay. So when I got over there, her boyfriend is there, and she went hollering and going on like I was doing something to her. The fellow told me to get out, and to prove his persistence he slapped me upside the head. I didn't have no idea nothing like this was gonna happen, but I always carried some kind of a weapon. I didn't have a gun but I did have what we used to call a Casey Mae, a bone-handle knife. And I upped with that and patted him pretty good with it.

That turned into a bad thing. I really thought the man was dead, but he'd didn't die, and I'm so glad. So that's what ended that thing right there. We hadn't got a divorce or nothing like that, but she was able to appear against me, which is unlawful because I hadn't done nothing to her. She tried to get as much as she could down there. I didn't fight it because I didn't care anyway. But it was no big deal. I appealed it and broke it down and it really didn't cost me no money because of the people I know. Then the divorce was coming, so I signed that right away. So that was the end of that episode.

After Nina and I fell out, I was still working for Independent Merchants, and this was how I met Vernell. Vernell was in debt with the company, and one of the other men had Vernell's credit. She was such a bad payer, she would pay but it was so ridiculous, she wouldn't even come halfway close to what she was supposed to pay. Anyway, she was turned over to me, and I started going after the money. She would give me something, and I found a way to get somewhere even.

I started going over there evenings. She said, "You come over and eat and I won't have to give you much money on your bill." I said, "I'll tell you what I'll do, maybe I'll just have to pay your bill." We got to kidding around with one another and it just went into an affair. What I'm saying is, I took over her and her debt!

We were together better than thirty years — we hit it off pretty good: sometimes she love me and sometimes she don't; sometimes she needs me if I call her and sometimes she won't. I would say our part had been more right than wrong. In each life there's rainfall, but I would say in our life there had been more harmony, especially in the beginning of it. It was more harmony than it was anything else. We had some pleasant moments together, and sometimes she wished I was in the kitchen and I wished she was downstairs somewhere. You know that goes on. So that killed my life with females; it was enough. I wouldn't want to relive none of that beginning part. I'm not sure with Vernell — maybe I would want to relive the beginning of ours. I think that was better than later, and she would have admit to that.[8]

It's kind of a rare thing to go into a ready-made family, go into it and survive — it's kinda rough. I knew it was rough when I went into it, but I knew I could handle me. I don't have any children from my marriages. My first wife, she couldn't carry — she was pregnant I don't know how many times. I think that was one of the things that kinda helped tear us apart. Even after we separated, the other man that she started living with, she got pregnant for him, but she couldn't hold it.

When I first come out of the service and after me and my first wife separated, my brother Minnow was married to a woman named Marie, and I met one of her sisters, and she just went crazy over me. Her husband was in the service and I started messing around with her and got her pregnant. That's the only kid. I don't know if I was the only guy there or not, but I know it panned out from the time period and everything. She told me right away — matter of fact, she told me when she thought she was. I was pretty close to her; there wasn't too much room for nobody else. Her daughter was born, and her husband came home about a few months after that, and she had him believe it was his, but she'd always tell me and laugh about it.

Years later the girl called me and asked me was I her father. And I really didn't have no choice but to tell her, since she called me and asked me that. I just told her, "Yes, so your mother said." I found out later that her mother had told my mother about it. The girl said the reason she kinda figured it out was because every time she would go to my brother's house, she had priority most of the time. So she asked her mother about it, and evidently her mother told her yes. But there was enough evidence there, because she was more or less like my side of the family. There was enough smoke there for a blaze to start.

* * *

I never did make a decision to give up music, but in the late 1950s I was just relaxed from it, and it remained that way because I found myself not interested. I never did toss it around in my mind whether I would go back or not, it just laid there in neutral for that period. I never actually gave up instruments that I had, and I was still active with my own self.

In 1959 I'd started working at Independent Merchants. Each person had their own thing in the store — the buying power was pooled and they bought up merchandise of all types; the store got 10 percent and the rest went to you. I was selling jewelry, furniture, clothes, shoes, you name it — everything.

I started off down there collecting debts — that's what you call a garbage man. I was real smooth at that debt collecting — people that didn't want to pay and all that. After that I went into the credit department, giving out qualified credits and whatnot. I was pretty good at that — feeling people's pulse without too much paperwork behind it or too much reference. I built myself up to where I was making some good money. And that's the reason I wasn't too involved in the music field.

Anyway, then along came Sam Charters. He asked me would I record, and I told him yes.[9] He wanted somebody to work with me as a bass and I couldn't locate nobody and his time was kinda running out. So I just called Tommy Bankhead and asked him did he want to do it and he said yes.[10]

We didn't even do a rehearsal, we just met in the studio. It was recorded at Technisonic studio. It wasn't too bad. See, I can play Bankhead's style and he can play my style real close. Way back Bankhead and I used to play exactly alike. He went on out to his thing later on, but he used to be almost in my tracks. See, I'm the guy that never done too much changing. I've stayed more or less with my style.

I wasn't necessarily overlooked as an artist in the early 1960s, but I'll tell you one of the reasons I wasn't involved as much as I could have been. My income here exceeded anything I could get out there. And rather than let it slip going into the music world, I preferred to hold on to it because I had "now" in mind. I had retiring in mind, and I was trying to build all the equity that I could, so that I would have enough when retirement time came.

I turned down some trips out of the States because the best offer I got was for two thousand dollars for an overseas deal — it wasn't no tour, just a onetime thing. If you turn down several things, it don't take long for the news to get around that he's not going. That was one thing I figured kept me from being involved with a lot of those things that were going on then. Locally I turned down a lot of college jobs, and they were local. George McCoy[11] was in there before I was and so was Clarence Johnson.[12] I was preoccupied, that's all there was to it.

The first time I was asked to go to Europe, they came looking for me on the job. The girl on the front desk thought that some police officers were looking for me — she didn't know that I was a musician. I asked her, "Who was it?" She said, "I don't know, they may have been FBI people or something! They said they were looking for you with some kind of music, but you don't play no music, do you?"

I done forgot who that was, but they were out of Europe. It was in the early sixties when they started bothering me about coming over there. I could have been in on the ground floor, but I didn't want to. It was way, way later when I come into it.[13] Later on I started going out into it pretty good, although I really didn't get into it until I retired when I was sixty-three years old, a little less than retirement age. That's when I went back into music heavily.

I never have built a mechanical formula where I feel this is the way a song should go. I guess the title of my documentary, *This Is The Way I Do It,* is pretty well all right.[14] It never was "this is the way that goes." Even the ones I attempt to make "this is the way that goes" don't pan out. "This is almost the way I done it before," that's the best I could say. I guess if you had a sample of me doing the same thing fifty times, if you look carefully you'd find it fifty different ways. But sincerely, the blues couldn't be nothing but a feeling coming from an individual, how you feel at that instant. This time I feel this way, the next time I feel slightly different.

My music has been a great big inspiration to me, and it has helped me to understand life. The sound of music has helped me to clarify problems that laid in the back of my mind that I couldn't solve. Now this might seem a little bit off the wall, but music is actually soothing to one that accepts sounds. And that's one of the reasons I've enjoyed music for so long.

But I write personal stuff from my experience — it's just something that ups and comes out. Chances are I didn't know what I was gonna say when I started off with it, I would just go ahead and do it. For instance, that song about, "you're having a good time now, / you're like the flower that comes in May, / but you got to remember you got to die some day." Another verse that I sing says, "man don't love that woman, / 'cause she don't love you and nobody else, / how in the world can she love you / when she don't even love herself." These things just come up and come out with me, always has.

But today I can't sing a single song all the way through that I've recorded. I don't know them and I never played my stuff back enough to learn them. I've always been aggressive going ahead with something else. That's not a nice thing for me, but that's the way it is. Like "Mistreated Blues" — I remember one or two verses and that's the size of it. If I was to do it now, I couldn't remember it. I would probably do it with new lyrics some kind of way. Whatever comes up to try and associate with whatever I was doing then.

I haven't been able to do a song the same way twice. I've got something written, but I'll tell you what, the little duet Vernell and I sang together, "Why Do We Love Each Other So," even that I don't do the same way. I even change the lyrics around in that. The tonic is the only thing we'd go together with, the theme of it.

Everybody's identified the minute they hit a string — you can't get away from that. If you know Henry Townsend and I hit a few strings, you'll know it's me without anybody telling you. Now that don't say that I don't play but one piece, it says that I have a trademark in my music that I can't leave. Chuck Berry does, so does B. B. King, and this is what it's all about.

But chances are everybody comes from somebody else. Somebody has to give you the inspiration to do what you're doing, so you have to give these people credit for enticing you to do what you're doing. Chuck Berry's thing come from T-Bone Walker; I stole them away from Lonnie Johnson. I tried to do like Lonnie Johnson — Lonnie done a whole lot of bending strings. He only quit when he started fooling with the twelve-string guitar. I steal them, but it don't sound like none of them. You can name any musician that's out there and I could name you somebody that they got it from. You're lucky when you can go to yourself, deviating from the other guy. You're lucky if you can stay far enough away from that to call yourself "yourself." You got to be pretty damn smart to do that, and there's not too many of us that can do it.

I have to brag about the type of education that I got, that I really needed or had to have in order to survive. I'm not ashamed to give myself credit for it, for fear nobody else don't! But you can make it. It's not easy, of course, and I wouldn't tell anybody that you don't need an education. So many times I regretted that I didn't have what I really needed. But through the years I learned to use what I got efficiently, and that helped me to survive and retain a living that was decent, at least satisfactory to me. Maybe not totally, but I didn't go to bed at night crying about what happened all that day.

I'm proud to say that down through the years the good and the bad that I had to face had been of value to me. Roosevelt and I used to talk about this all the time, that "the great success has never been mine." Now I'm not sure whether it's yes or no. But to think of it in detail, maybe it was the best way. How do I know if success would have been overwhelming? My desire in life was not to be the greatest person in the world, to get so far to the sky I could look down on everything. I never had that desire.

A few years ago I received an award from the National Endowment for the Arts.[15] That was nice. I guess it's about the nicest thing that ever happened to me, in essence. I didn't have to perform at all, although I did do something. That was one of the better things that happened to me in my entire life in the music field.

But I don't have a whole lot of regrets for what I've done. Some things that I felt I should have done more about, and it wasn't totally my ignorance. I guess Roosevelt and I had a lot in common like that. I knew better. A lot of things that I went ahead with wasn't because I didn't know better, it's something I wanted to do and I said, "Well, so what?" That could have been rewarding for the credit that I got, for being who I am. But I don't regret it. Not a lot.

Let me say something. Your life is the life you live. What you live is how it should be written. If it hurts, it's too late anyway. Whatever you done, it's too late to try and fix it or patch it. Can't nobody put nobody nowhere, heaven or hell, across the field or into the corn patch. If you lived it, you lived it — making it pretty don't help a bit.

A lot of people think what I'm doing is a terrible sin. I don't think so. I heard somebody say Muddy Waters just sung his way to hell. How do they know where he sung his way to? I don't sing lies, and a tune sure can't condemn you. Now it depends on the purpose in this person's heart: "Oh it's all right, it's the truth, but you're doing it for the Devil." Who said who I'm doing it for, the Devil or God? What tells you I'm doing it for the Devil? I don't want nobody to make my funeral look pretty; make it look like the life I lived. That's all.

NOTES

Chapter 1: "Like a Bullet"

1. According to other sources, Henry Townsend lived in Future City.
2. By the late 1940s, E. Benjamin Koonce owned a large funeral home that boasted a fleet of Packard limousines and a hearse that featured "sacred chimes." The business was located at 1221 North Grand Boulevard, which today is the site of Ted Foster's Funeral Home.
3. Jordan Chambers, a well-known democratic politician, owned People's Undertaking Company at 3100 Franklin Avenue. He is perhaps best remembered as the owner of the Riviera, located on Delmar near Taylor. The Riviera was one of St. Louis's best-known night clubs. Opening its doors in June 1944, it continued to operate through the sixties, when a fire destroyed the building. Jordan Chambers died in August 1962.
4. Many whites believed that employers in the East St. Louis meatpacking, iron, and steel industries imported cheap black labor to break strikes. This was but one of the many reasons for unrest leading up to the 1917 riot.

   White ignorance and prejudice manifested itself when delegates from various unions appeared before the mayor and city council on 28 May to protest black migration. Following the meeting an angry mob took to the street, attacking and beating any black person in its path.

   Inflammatory statements in the press and the harassment of blacks continued throughout the following month. The riot eventually erupted on 2 July. Due to East St. Louis's inadequate municipal records, the exact number of blacks who lost their lives is unknown, although the total was at least thirty-nine. The county coroner recorded only that nine whites had been killed.
5. The Booker Washington Theatre, located at 2248 Market Street, was owned and operated by Charles H. Turpin. The theater was one of the first in the United States to be owned by and to cater to black people. With a seating capacity of one thousand, the Booker Washington was in operation from about 1912 to 1930 and featured a new show each week. The black stars Bessie Smith, Ma Rainey, and Clara Smith often appeared at the theater, which was also on the Theater Owners' Booking Association (TOBA) circuit (the organization was also referred to, rather derisively, by many of the artists who worked for it as "Tough on Black Asses").

   Turpin, who was probably born in 1873, was also involved in St. Louis politics. He was the first St. Louis black man to be elected to a local office. Running as a candidate for the Independent Citizen's Liberty League, he was elected constable in 1910. In 1928, he was elected justice of the peace and he was reelected in 1934. Turpin was also a pioneer in filmmaking, supervising the filming of events involving black people. Turpin died in December 1935.

6. This is possibly the Bekins Moving and Storage Company, which has been in business in St. Louis since 1891.

Chapter 2: "The Sweetest Guitar I've Ever Played"

1. City Hospital Number Two, located on Lawton, was the hospital for black people. City Hospital Number One was for whites.

2. Henry Townsend was living at 1819 Biddle Street when he was arrested by Sergeant Thomas Davis and Patrolman Walter Promintz of the Fourth District on 13 December 1926. The charge was "Delinquent, by larceny."

   Sgt. Davis's report is as follows: "About 1:40 o'clock this p.m., Patrolman Promintz arrested in the junk yard at 1900 Wash St., conducted by Sam Kohn, one Henry Townsend, colored, 17 years old, son of Allen and Amelia Townsend, residing at 1818 (?) Biddle St, and Louis Brent, colored, 32 years old, single, a laborer, living at 2912 Thomas St; on complaint made by Sam Fenster, residing at 2834 Thomas St, who says that he had seen Townsend take two junk batteries valued at $3.00 from his wagon which was in front of his home at 2834 Thomas St. and load them into Bent's [*sic*] wagon. Larry D. Davis, of Route No. 2, Box 355 Olive St. Road, Clayton, Missouri, state that they had seen Brent and the Townsend boy take the batteries and load them into the wagon owned by Brent. The batteries were not found in their possession when arrested. Brent is being held at this station, pending an application of a warrant. The Townsend boy will be turned over to his parents, with instructions to have him appear in court when notified."

3. The tornado hit the town on 30 September 1927.

4. Morgan Street is now Delmar Avenue.

5. Lonnie Johnson, "St. Louis Cyclone Blues," Okeh 8512, 3 October 1927.

6. Wolff's Music Shop was at 1319 Biddle Street.

7. The owner of Joe's Music operated several record stores in St. Louis throughout the years. One store was still located at the corner of Kingshighway and Page in 1994.

8. Henry Spaulding, "Cairo Blues"/"Biddle Street Blues," Brunswick 7085, 9 May 1929. Spaulding, who was reputedly from Mississippi, worked as

a barber with a shop on Biddle Street. He is thought to have died in 1938.

9. Franklin is now Dr. Martin Luther King Drive.
10. Pete Bogans died in 1990.
11. After years of struggling to secure a championship bout, thirty nine year-old Archie Moore won the world light heavyweight title by defeating Joey Maxim at the St. Louis arena on 17 December 1952. Archie Moore held the light heavyweight crown for over nine years. In a career that spanned the years 1936 to 1963, Archie was 183-22-9, scoring 129 knockouts, the most in history.
12. The visit was circa 1986.

Chapter 3: "Revenge Is Sweet"

1. Kinloch is located in north St. Louis County approximately fifteen miles from the downtown St. Louis. Then as now, the municipality has a predominantly black population. In recent years much of Kinloch has been swallowed up by the expansion of Lambert Field.
2. The Dance Box, located at 210 North Ewing, was in operation during the late twenties and thirties. Clara Smith performed there in early June 1929. In March 1935 the night spot was still going strong, featuring music by the St. Louis Crackerjacks.
3. By "classics" Henry means the popular songs of the day.
4. Henry means homosexual.
5. Luella Miller, "Dago Hill Blues"/"Pretty Man Blues," Vocalion 1044, 7 July 1926.
6. Dago Hill, today known as the Hill, is an Italian neighborhood in south St. Louis.
7. An Al Miller played guitar on some of Luella Miller's records. He also recorded as Al Miller and His Market Street Boy's, which would also suggest a St. Louis connection.
8. Irene Scruggs was born in Mississippi on 7 December 1901 and was raised in St. Louis. In February 1924, Okeh Records sponsored a blues talent contest at the Booker Washington Theatre. Irene won first prize, which was a recording contract. Between 1924 and 1930 she recorded quite prolifically with both jazz and blues accompanists, including a session with Tampa Red. She remained active in music into the midthirties, when she returned to St. Louis. However, she would still tour with her daughter, the shake dancer Baby Scruggs.

In 1953 Irene appeared at the NFJO Jazz Band Ball in London, En-

gland, also appearing on "Ballads and Blues" on BBC Radio. She reportedly settled in Paris, France, and then in Germany in the seventies.

9. The DeLuxe Music Shoppe was located at 2234 Market Street and was
owned by Jesse Johnson. Johnson, a prominent black businessman, was
born in Clarksville, Tennessee, on 12 May 1883. In the early 1900s the
family, which included his brother, the pianist James "Stump" Johnson,
moved to St. Louis. Johnson opened his DeLuxe Music Shoppe in 1919.
In 1925 he married Edith North, who went on to have her own career
as Edith Johnson.

Throughout the 1920s Johnson, using his position in the community,
acted as a talent scout for several record companies. He was directly responsible for many artists first appearing on recordings, including
Roosevelt Sykes and Victoria Spivey. Johnson's other activities included
the promotion of dances at ballrooms and aboard riverboat steamers. He
also managed the St. Louis and midwestern bookings of many popular
big bands, including those of Louis Armstrong, Jimmy Lunceford, and
Duke Ellington. Jesse Johnson also diversified his business. In May 1935
he and Edith opened the DeLuxe Restaurant at 10 North Jefferson. The
restaurant was soon followed by a fleet of DeLuxe Taxi Cabs. By 1944
there was a Hotel DeLuxe located at Enright and Walton, managed by
his brother, Stump. Jesse Johnson died on 15 February 1946.

10. Victoria Spivey's "Black Snake Blues," Okeh 8338, was recorded in St.
Louis on 11 May 1926.

11. Henry Townsend and Sylvester Palmer recorded on 15 November 1929.

12. Sylvester Palmer died on 8 May 1930. His death certificate yields very
few clues. His date of birth is given as "about 1901" and his birthplace
as "Illinois." At the time of his death he was living at 3163 Clark Street
in St. Louis. Palmer's occupation is listed as "musician." These few scant
details were presumably supplied by "Amanda," who is listed as his wife.

13. The pianist Wesley Wallace had only two sides issued under his own
name, "Fanny Lee Blues"/"No. 29," Paramount 12958, circa November
1929. Wallace also accompanied the vocalists Robert Peeples and Bessie
Mae Smith on their Paramount sides.

The date of Wallace's arrival in St. Louis is unknown. On 20 May
1922, however, he was arrested along with ten others at 408 South Fourteenth Street and was charged with suspicion of gambling. Wallace, who
was living at 111 North Thirteenth Street, gave his age as thirty and his
birthplace as Tennessee.

14. The area around Third Street was leveled for the construction of inter-
state highways 55 and 64.

15. According to Dixon and Godrich in *Blues and Gospel Records, 1902–43*,

Oscar Carter accompanied Sykes on his first session for Okeh Records on 14 June 1929. Henry could only vaguely recall Carter: "I didn't know Oscar Carter real well. I know of Oscar, but I never did know him. He mingled around, he was with Sykes some to my knowledge. I heard Roosevelt talk about him." Clifford Gibson did record for QRS Records in New York circa June 1929, one of his numbers being "Tired of Being Mistreated," parts 1 and 2. It is possible that Sykes and Gibson traveled together to these sessions. Gibson also recorded with Sykes for Victor Records on 9 June 1931. Walter Sykes recorded two sides for Okeh Records on 17 November 1929. "I Won't Be Long Blues"/"Unkind Blues" remain unissued.

16. Henry Townsend, "All I've Got's Gone," Bluebird 7474, 11 November 1937.

17. Charlie McFadden first recorded "Groceries on the Shelf," Paramount 12928, in 1929 accompanied by Roosevelt Sykes. As Henry stated, it was probably his most popular number, as he subsequently rerecorded the song at three other sessions.

18. According to the St. Louis Police Department files, Charles McFadden was born in 1895 in Illinois. Between 1929 and 1935 he was arrested a total of twelve times for suspected larceny, violating the bone dry law, and gambling. At the time of his last arrest on 6 May 1935, he was living at 1926 North Fifteenth Street. Charlie McFadden last recorded on 30 April 1937.

19. J. D. Short was born in Port Gibson, Mississippi, on 26 December 1902, moved to St. Louis in the early twenties, and soon established himself as a popular local artist. In the early thirties Short recorded for both Paramount and Vocalion Records and pseudonymously for Bluebird and quite possibly Victor Records. Short continued to work in and around St. Louis but did not record again under his own name until a few months before his death in October 1962.

Chapter 4: "Have Fun with It"

1. Paramount Records was a subsidiary of the Wisconsin Chair Company of Port Washington, Wisconsin.

2. Henry Thomas (Townsend), "My Sweet Candy," Bluebird 5343, 11 December 1933.

3. Henry Townsend's early recordings have been reissued on numerous blues anthologies. See the discography for details.

4. Henry Townsend, "Jack of Diamonds Georgia Rub"/"Doctor, Oh Doc-

tor," Paramount 13097, circa 1931. No copies of this record were known to exist until one surfaced in January 1995.

5. The former St. Louis bandleader Eddie Randle was the owner of a funeral home at 4600 Natural Bridge.

6. Oliver Cobb was a popular St. Louis trumpet player and bandleader. As Cobb was primarily a jazz artist, his jobs were advertised in the *St. Louis Argus*, unlike those of his blues counterparts. The last advertised job I could find for Cobb was 7 December 1930, when he was scheduled to play at the Paradise Dance Palace, at Sarah and Hodiamont Tracks. Under the headline "Brunswick Recording Orchestra Re-organized," the 2 January 1931 issue of the *St. Louis Argus* published the following:

> Due to illness Oliver Cobbs [*sic*] former leader of the Brunswick Recording Orchestra has resigned his leadership and a permanent organization has been formed.
>
> Ed Johnson, pianist and arranger, is the new leader and the name of the band has been changed to the Crackerjacks. These boys have been together for four years and have made an enviable record among both white and colored in the states of Missouri, Illinois, Arkansas and Tennessee.
>
> James Telphy, recently of the Salt and Pepper Shakers, fills the vacancy made by Cobbs.

Dixon and Godrich in *Blues and Gospel Records, 1902–43* give an approximate date for Cobb's Paramount Session as 1 June 1930 and Henry Townsend's session as May 1931. Henry Townsend, Oliver Cobb, Roosevelt Sykes, Charlie McFadden, Edith Johnson, and possibly Red Mike Bailey all recorded at the same session. Cobb's June 1930 session and Henry Townsend's May 1931 session are probably one and the same.

If Cobb died as a result of a swimming accident in Lake Michigan as Henry claims, the time period would suggest the summer months. No mention of Cobb's activities can be found after December 1930. The probable date of the Paramount session is summer 1931.

7. Dixon and Godrich, in *Blues and Gospel Records, 1902–43* list Edith Johnson as the pianist on Oliver Cobb's Paramount session.

8. St. Louis Red Mike Bailey recorded for Paramount in 1931 possibly accompanied by Roosevelt Sykes.

9. Walter Davis, "M and O Blues," Victor 38618, 12 June 1930.

10. The Victor Records session was on 9 June 1931.

11. According to Dixon and Godrich in *Blues and Gospel Records, 1902–43*, Minnow Townsend recorded "Pistol Shy Blues"/"Staggering Blues," Victor Records, 9 June 1931. Both titles remain unissued.

12. Willie Kelly (Roosevelt Sykes), "True as I've Been to You," Victor 23286, 9 June 1931.

13. Willie Kelly (Roosevelt Sykes), "Hard Luck Man Blues," Victor 23320, 9 June 1931.

14. By the "entertaining field" Henry means popular songs.

15. The Ville is a north St. Louis neighborhood bounded on the north by St. Louis Avenue, on the east by Sarah Street, on the south by Dr. Martin Luther King Drive (formerly Easton), and on the west by Taylor Avenue.

    Clifford Gibson did indeed live further west of downtown than many of his contemporaries. When he was arrested on a suspicion of gambling charge on 24 October 1926, he was living at 3337 Laclede Avenue and gave his age as twenty-four.

16. Georgia Boyd, "Never Mind Blues"/"I'm Sorry Blues," Bluebird 5573, 2 August 1933. Boyd was accompanied by J. D. Short on guitar for "Never Mind Blues" and Roosevelt Sykes on piano for "I'm Sorry Blues."

    Apart from the few details Henry provides, very little else is know about Georgia Boyd. She was arrested twice in 1925. The first occasion was on 1 May for violating the state Prohibition law. Boyd gave her age as twenty-two and said she was a native of Missouri. At the time of her arrest she was living at 2900 Lucas Avenue and listed her occupation as "none." Her next brush with the law was on 2 November. No address was given on this occasion, but her occupation was listed as "prostitute" and she was sent to the "Health Department."

17. Dorothea Trowbridge, "Bad Luck Blues"/"Slavin' Mama Blues," Bluebird 5431, 2 August 1933. Dorothea was accompanied by Pinetop Sparks on piano.

18. Isabel Sykes, "I'm Here with Your Heavy Stuff"/"Don't Rush Yourself," Bluebird 5170, 2 August 1933. Isabel was accompanied by Roosevelt Sykes on piano.

19. Despite Henry's claim of Edith Johnson being at the session, no titles have ever surfaced.

20. Napoleon Fletcher, "Mr. Fletcher's Blues" (unissued), "She Showed It All," Bluebird 5383, 11 December 1933. Fletcher was accompanied by Roosevelt Sykes on piano.

21. Carl Rafferty, "Dresser with the Drawers"/"Mr. Carl's Blues," Bluebird 5429, 11 December 1933. Rafferty was accompanied by Roosevelt Sykes on piano.

22. Bessie Mae Smith, aka St. Louis Bessie, recorded a total of nineteen sides between the years 1927 and 1930 for Okeh, Paramount, and Vocalion Records.

23. Alice Moore, "Black and Evil Blues," Paramount 12819, 16 August 1929. Alice Moore recorded quite prolifically for Paramount and Decca Records between 1929 and 1937. As with so many other St. Louis art-

ists, details of her life are scant. She was previously thought to have been born in St. Louis in 1903. In March 1925 Alice was arrested twice. The first occasion was on 7 March for "suspicion of gambling." She gave her address as 2016 Walnut Street, her age as twenty-one, and her birthplace as Tennessee. Her occupation was listed as "housework." She was arrested again on 27 March, although instead of being charged she was sent to the "Health Department." Alice was living at 2118 Randolph Street when on 19 September 1926 she was arrested and charged with "disturbing the peace."

24. A popular figure in the late twenties and thirties, the pianist Joe Dean was born in St. Louis on 25 April 1908, one of the few local blues artists who originated in the city. As Joe Dean (from Bowling Green) he recorded "I'm So Glad I'm Twenty One Years Old Today"/"Mexico Bound Blues," Vocalion 1544, circa July 1930. An excellent example of St. Louis style piano blues, this was unfortunately Joe's only excursion into the studio. Joe Dean remained musically active, albeit on a part-time basis, into the sixties. Retiring in 1972 after twenty-three years at Granite City Steel, he became the Rev. Joe Dean at St. John's United Church of Christ on North Grand. Joe Dean died on 24 June 1981.

25. Barrelhouse Buck and Peetie Wheatstraw recorded together for Decca Records in August 1934. Buck McFarland was living at 2319A Carr in 1936.

26. This is possibly Willie Fields.

27. Peetie Wheatstraw died in an automobile accident in East St. Louis on 21 December 1941.

28. Jabo Williams was reputedly from Birmingham, Alabama. In May 1932 he recorded eight sides for Paramount Records. Very little else is known of him.

   On 3 January 1934, the St. Louis police arrested several people at the Blue Heaven, at 1416 North Jefferson Avenue, for violating the state bone dry law. Among those arrested was a Jab Williams, age twenty-six, of 1342 Elliot. Williams gave his birthplace as Texas.

29. Marion (Milton) Sparks was charged with manslaughter following an argument during which he stabbed Edward Randolph at William Taylor's dance hall at 930 North Twenty-second Street on 23 August 1936. The case came to trial on 16 April 1937. After pleading guilty, Milton was sentenced to six months in the city workhouse.

30. Henry Brown and Ike Rogers recorded together in 1929 for both Brunswick and Paramount Records. The pair also accompanied Mary Johnson and Alice Moore on sides for Brunswick, Paramount, and Decca Records.

Chapter 5: "The Music Is a Mind Disturber"

1. Following years of argument during which twenty-five states passed their own Prohibition laws, the Eighteenth Amendment was passed into law, and beer, wine, and liquor were officially banned on 16 January 1920. The unpopular law was eventually repealed on 5 December 1933.
2. The 1936 St. Louis street directory lists Ernest Walker's address as 1118 Jefferson.
3. Robert Johnson, "Terraplane Blues," ARC 7-03-56/Vocalion 03416, 23 November 1936.
4. During the midthirties vocalist/guitarist Charley Jordan operated a rehearsal hall and acted as a talent scout for Decca Records. One of the major artists on the St. Louis scene, Jordan recorded prolifically for both Vocalion and Decca records.

    Details of Jordan's life are at best sketchy. He suffered from paralysis of the lower body, the result of a gunshot wound to his spine in 1924. Charley Jordan's birthplace has been given variously as Memphis, Tennessee, and Mabelvale, Arkansas circa 1890. The date of Jordan's arrival in St. Louis is also unknown.

    On 5 July 1926 Jordan was living at 1128A (rear) North Twelfth Street. Following an argument with a Lizzie Turner, during which she pointed a gun at him, Jordan shot her dead. He was subsequently charged with murder. In a statement to the police he gave his age as thirty years old and his birthplace as Mississippi.

    Jordan did not record again after 1937 and he died in Homer G. Phillips Hospital in St. Louis on 15 November 1954.
5. "Hi" Henry Brown recorded a total of six sides for Vocalion between 14 and 17 March 1932. The identity of "Hi" Henry Brown has never been established, but he should not be confused with the pianist Henry Brown.
6. "Hi" Henry Brown, "Nut Factory Blues," Vocalion 1692, 17 March 1932.
7. Another blues enigma is the vocalist/guitar player Lane Hardin. Hardin was born in Tennessee in 1897. By September 1920 he was living at 410 North Levee. Hardin also had two brothers, William and Grady, living in St. Louis.

    It would also appear that Lane was a gambling man, for between the years 1920 and 1925 he was arrested no fewer than eleven times for gambling offenses. He also changed addresses frequently, as his various addresses for this period were 405 North Levee, 407 North Levee, 409 North Levee, 410 North Levee, 125 Elm, and 1608 Morgan. By 1925 he had married a woman named Edith. In September 1930 Hardin was living at 1727 Biddle Street. The following year he had moved to 1631 Carr. His addresses until September 1934 were 2037 Biddle, 2841 Thomas, and 2732 Thomas.

It has been suggested that Lane Hardin also recorded during the fifties, but this remains unproven.

8. Lane Hardin, "Hard Time Blues"/"California Desert Blues," Bluebird 6242, 28 July 1935.

9. Henry Townsend, Walter Davis, and Big Joe Williams recorded for Bluebird Records on 25 February 1935 following a session by Leroy Carr and Scrapper Blackwell.

10. Leroy Carr, "How Long – How Long Blues," Vocalion 1191, 19 June 1928. "Prison Bound Blues," Vocalion 1241, 20 December 1928.

11. Singer/songwriter St. Louis Jimmy was born James Burke Oden in Nashville, Tennessee, on 26 June 1903 and moved to St. Louis in 1917. With his laid-back, half-spoken vocals, St. Louis Jimmy recorded for a myriad of labels throughout a career that began in the midtwenties. Moving to Chicago in the early forties, he scored his biggest hit with the classic "Going Down Slow." His real claim to fame, however, was as one of the major songwriters of the blues genre, with dozens of widely recorded compositions to his credit. St. Louis Jimmy died in Chicago on 30 December 1977.

12. St. Louis Jimmy, "Going Down Slow," Bluebird 8889, 11 November 1941. Jimmy was accompanied by Roosevelt Sykes on piano.

13. Henry Townsend accompanied Big Joe Williams on his first recording session for Bluebird Records on 25 February 1935.

14. The guitarist Pete Bogans also thought the victim's name was Willie White. Although Henry or Pete Bogans could not recall the exact date of the incident, it is thought to have taken place sometime during the thirties.

15. Walter Davis, "M and O Blues," Victor 38618, 12 June 1930.

16. Davis was born in Grenada, Mississippi.

17. Walter Davis died in St. Louis on 22 October 1963.

18. On Walter Davis's early sessions he was accompanied by Roosevelt Sykes on piano.

19. Music publisher, talent scout, and record company executive Lester Melrose was responsible for recording a large proportion of the artists for RCA and Columbia Records between 1934 and 1951.

20. In late 1947 Walter Davis brought a civil action dating back to the years 1935–36 for nonpayment of royalties on twenty-two songs. The case was brought against RCA Victor, Lester Melrose, and Eli Oberstein, who

was then the A&R man with RCA. The case was apparently settled amicably, since Davis recorded a session for RCA on 27 July 1952.

21. A birthdate of 1 March 1912 has always been given for Walter Davis. However, since much of Henry Townsend's information on Davis contradicts previously published information, it comes as no surprise that his date of birth is also in question.

    A biography of Davis issued 30 March 1953 by the publicity department of RCA Victor following the release of "Tears Came Rollin' Down" gives a birthdate of 1 March 1909. If Davis did record as a minor, this may help to explain the confusion — or subterfuge — about his birthdate.

22. Walter Davis and Henry Townsend recorded for Bullet Records in Nashville, Tennessee, in 1949 and 1950. Several St. Louis and former St. Louis artists also recorded for Bullet, including Roosevelt Sykes, Big Joe Williams, and St. Louis Jimmy.

23. Henry Townsend's composition, "Tears Came Rollin' Down," RCA Victor 20–5012, was recorded at Walter Davis's last session on 27 July 1952.

24. John Lee "Sonny Boy" Williamson was born in Jackson, Tennessee, on 30 March 1914. From the late thirties until his untimely death on 1 June 1948, he made his home in Chicago.

25. Washboard Sam recorded for Bluebird Records on 11 November 1937, the same day as Henry Townsend, Walter Davis, Sonny Boy Williamson, and Robert Lee McCoy.

26. Robert Lee McCoy (Robert Nighthawk), "Brickyard," Bluebird 7416, 11 November 1937.

27. Roosevelt Sykes, "Red Eyed Jesse Bell," Delmark DL-607, May 1963. This number is musically similar to "West Helena Blues."

28. Speckled Red, "The Dirty Dozen," Brunswick 7116, 22 September 1929.

29. Rufus Perryman, aka Speckled Red, was born in Monroe, Louisiana, on 23 October 1892. Red's adolescent years were spent in Georgia and Detroit before he hit the road to lead the life of an itinerant musician. After spending some time in Memphis, he eventually settled in St. Louis in the late thirties, working the taverns and clubs. Red was also a fixture in the clubs of Gaslight Square during the fifties. He was also a member of the select group of blues artists to first tour England and Europe in the late fifties. Pre–World War II sessions for Brunswick and Bluebird Records and albums for Delmark and Storyville make up this wonderfully eccentric and boisterous pianist's legacy. Speckled Red died in St. Louis on 2 January 1973.

30. Between the years 1950 and 1953, Memphis Slim and Matt Murphy spent a considerable amount of time in St. Louis. The pair played extended

engagements at the Show Bar, the Chesterfield Bar on Eighteenth and Franklin, the Glass Bar on Lawton, and the Barn on Finney.

Chapter 6: "A Very Good Hustle"

1. Otha/Othum Brown was a guitar player and an early partner of Little Walter. The pair recorded for Chicago's Ora Nelle Records in 1947.
2. Jew Town was otherwise known as Maxwell Street Market and was located in and around the Maxwell and Halsted area of Chicago.
3. Eddie El was a guitar player.
4. Eddie Boyd first recorded on 3 April 1947.
5. Amos Easton, aka Bumble Bee Slim, recorded prolifically for Paramount Vocalion, Bluebird, and Decca Records throughout the thirties.
6. James "Kokomo" Arnold was an influential slide guitarist.
7. Henry Townsend and Robert Jr. Lockwood worked together at the 1984 World's Fair in New Orleans.
8. Former Radio KATZ disk jockey Gabriel leased the Majestic Theater on Collinsville Avenue in East St. Louis in the late sixties. The Muddy Waters Band and Henry Townsend appeared there on 8 February 1969.
9. The Grand Central, the Calumet, the West End, and the Albany Hotels were all owned by Maurice Mushlin.

Chapter 7: "Making It Pretty Don't Help a Bit"

1. The West End Waiters at 911 North Vandeventer Avenue opened its doors on 24 December 1942 and continued in business into the early sixties.
2. The Glass Bar, located in the Midtown Hotel at 2935 Lawton, began operation in November 1944.
3. Clayton is a suburb west of downtown St. Louis.
4. Joe Willie Wilkins was born 7 January 1923 and died 28 March 1979.
5. Henry Townsend, "Tired of Being Mistreated," Bluesville BVLP 1041, 17 May 1961.
6. Aleck "Rice" Miller, aka Sonny Boy Williamson, was reportedly born in Glendora, Mississippi, on 5 December 1899 and died in Helena, Arkansas, on 25 May 1965. Miller first recorded in 1951, fourteen years after John Lee Williams's recording debut.
7. Albert King moved to St. Louis from Osceola, Arkansas, in 1956.
8. Vernell Townsend died on 21 September 1995.

9. Sam Charters is a record producer, a musicologist, and an author.
10. The vocalist and guitar player Tommy Bankhead has been resident in St. Louis since 1949.
11. Guitar-playing brother and sister George and Ethel McCoy were the nephew and niece of Memphis Minnie through her marriage to Joe McCoy.
12. The East St. Louis vocalist/guitarist Clarence Johnson is reputedly the son of Lonnie Johnson.
13. Henry Townsend did not visit Europe until 1980.
14. *This Is the Way I Do It* is a 1986 video documentary on the life of Henry Townsend by Cathy Corley.
15. Henry Townsend was the recipient of a National Heritage Award from the National Endowment for the Arts in 1985.

DISCOGRAPHY

The following is a chronological listing of Henry Townsend's recordings as both featured artist and accompanist. Only the original issue numbers are listed.

HENRY TOWNSEND
vcl/gtr
Chicago, Ill. 15 Nov. 1929

403300-A	Henry's Worry Blues	Columbia 14529-D
403301-A	Mistreated Blues	Columbia 14491-D
403302-A-B	Long Ago Blues	Columbia 14529-D
403302-A	Poor Man Blues	Columbia 14591-D

HENRY TOWNSEND
vcl/gtr
Grafton, Wisc. prob. summer 1931

L464-1	Doctor, Oh Doctor	Paramount 13097
L469-1	Jack of Diamonds Georgia Rub	Paramount 13097

WILLIE KELLY (Roosevelt Sykes)
vcl/pno; Henry Townsend, gtr-1; Clifford Gibson, gtr-2
Louisville, Ky. 9 June 1931

69400-2	Sunshine Special Blues	Victor Unissued
69401-1	No Settled Mind Blues	Victor 23320
69402-2	Hard Rock Was My Pillow	Victor Unissued
69403-1	True as I've Been to You-1	Victor 23286
69404-1	Hard Luck Man Blues-2	Victor 23320

MINNOW TOWNSEND (Lazarus Townsend)
vcl; Willie Kelly (Roosevelt Sykes) pno; Henry Townsend, gtr-1
Louisville, Ky. 9 June 1931

69407-2	Pistol Shy Blues	Victor Unissued
69418-2	Staggering Blues-1	Victor Unissued

JESSE TOWNSEND (Henry Townsend)
vcl/gtr; Willie Kelly (Roosevelt Sykes), pno
Louisville, Ky. 9 June 1931

69410-2	No Home Blues	Victor 23322
69411-2	Take a Chance	Victor 23322

WALTER DAVIS

vcl; Willie Kelly (Roosevelt Sykes), pno; Henry Townsend, gtr-1

Louisville, Ky. 9 June 1931

69414-1	Railroad Man Blues-1	Victor 23291
69415-1	You Don't Worry My Mind-1	Victor 23291
69416-2	That Stuff You Sell Ain't No Good	Victor 23282
69417-1	What Made Me Love You So?	Victor 23282

HENRY THOMAS (Henry Townsend)

vcl/gtr; Roosevelt Sykes, pno-1

Chicago, Ill. 11 December 1933

77309-1	Can't Do That No More-1	Bluebird Unn.
77310-1	She's Got What I Want-1	Bluebird B5343
77311-1	My Sweet Candy-1	Bluebird B5343
77314-1	Sick with the Blues	Bluebird B5411

WALTER DAVIS

vcl/pno; Joe Williams, gtr; Henry Townsend, gtr-1

Chicago, Ill. 25 February 1935

85479-1	Sloppy Drunk Again-1	Bluebird B5879
85480-1	Travelin' This Lonesome Road-1	Bluebird B5982
85481-1	Sad and Lonesome Blues-1	Bluebird B5982
85482-1	Minute Man Blues pt. 1-1	Bluebird B5969
85483-1	Minute Man Blues pt. 2-1	Bluebird B5969
85484-1	Sweet Sixteen-1	Bluebird B5931
85485-1	Wonder Where My Baby's Gone-1	Bluebird B5879
85486-1	Lay around on Your DBA	Bluebird B5931

JOE WILLIAMS

vcl/gtr; Henry Townsend, gtr-1

Chicago, Ill. 25 February 1935

85487-1	Little Leg Woman	Bluebird B5900
85488-1	Somebody's Been Borrowing That Stuff-1	Bluebird B5900
85489-1	Providence Help the Poor People	Bluebird B5930
85490-1	49 Highway Blues	Bluebird B5996
85491-1	My Grey Pony	Bluebird B5948
85492-2	Stepfather Blues	Bluebird B5996

HENRY TOWNSEND
vcl/gtr
Chicago, Ill. 25 February 1935

85493-1	Don't Love That Woman	Bluebird B5966
85494-1	She's Got a Mean Disposition	Bluebird B5966

WALTER DAVIS
vcl/pno; Henry Townsend, gtr
Chicago, Ill. 28 July 1935

91429-1	Dentist Blues	Bluebird B6040
91430-1	Root Man Blues	Bluebird B6040
91431-1	Pearly May	Bluebird B6074
91432-1	What Have I Done Wrong?	Bluebird B6074
91433-1	I Can Tell by the Way You Smell	Bluebird B6059
91434-1	Santa Claus	Bluebird B6125

PINETOP (Aaron Sparks)
vcl/pno; Henry Townsend, gtr-1
Chicago, Ill. 28 July 1935

91439-1	Tell Her about Me-1	Bluebird B6529
91440-1	Every Day I Have the Blues-1	Bluebird B5621
91441-1	Got the Blues about My Baby-1	Bluebird B6096
91442-1	Workhouse Blues	Bluebird B6126

MILTON SPARKS
vcl; Aaron Sparks, pno-1; Walter Davis, pno-2; Henry Townsend, gtr
Chicago, Ill. 28 July 1935

91445-1	Erie Train Blues-2	Bluebird B6529
91446-1	Ina Blues-2	Bluebird B6521
91447-1	Grinder Blues-1	Bluebird B6096
91448-1	I Wake Up in the Morning	Bluebird B6126

WALTER DAVIS
vcl/pno; Henry Townsend, gtr
Chicago, Ill. 31 October 1935

96234-1	Moonlight Is My Spread	Bluebird B6167
96235-1	Don't the Clouds Look Lonesome?	Bluebird B6167
96236-1	Katy Blues	Bluebird B6201
96237-1	Ashes in My Whiskey	Bluebird B6201
96238-1	Blues at Midnight	Bluebird B6228
96239-1	Can't Get along with You	Bluebird B6228

WALTER DAVIS
vcl/pno-1; Henry Townsend, gtr; Robert Lee McCoy, gtr/vcl-2
Aurora, Ill. 5 May 1937

07641-1	Angel Child-1	Bluebird B7064
07642-1	Fifth Avenue Blues-1	Bluebird B7021
07643-1	I Ain't Got Changing Cloths	Bluebird B7021
07644-1	West Coast Blues-1	Bluebird B7064
07645-1	Shady Lane-1	Bluebird B6996
07646-1	What Else Can I Do?-1	Bluebird B6971
07647-1	Nightmare Blues-1	Bluebird B6971
07648-1	Good Gal-2	Bluebird B6996

WALTER DAVIS
vcl/pno; Henry Townsend, gtr
Aurora, Ill. 11 November 1937

016510-1	Holiday Blues	Bluebird B7329
016511-1	Let Me Dig Your Basement	unissued
016512-1	Streamline Woman	Bluebird B7329
016513-1	Let Me Meg Your Water	unissued
016514-1	Big Jack Engine Blues	Bluebird B7375
016515-1	Guiding Rod	Bluebird B7292
016516-1	Talk's All over Town	Bluebird B7292
016517-1	My Babe	Bluebird B7375

SONNY BOY WILLIAMSON
vcl/hra; Robert Lee McCoy or Henry Townsend, gtr
Aurora, Ill. 11 November 1937

016518	Up the Country Blues	Bluebird B7428
016519	Worried Me Blues	Bluebird B7404
016520	Black Gal Blues	Bluebird B7352
016521	Collector Man Blues	Bluebird B7428
016522	Frigidaire Blues	Bluebird B7404
016523	Suzanna Blues	Bluebird B7352
016524	Early in the Morning	Bluebird B7302
016525	Project Highway	Bluebird B7302

ROBERT LEE MCCOY
vcl/gtr; poss Sonny Boy Williamson, hra-1; Henry Townsend, pno-2/gtr-3; Joe Williams, gtr
Aurora, Ill. 11 November 1937

| 016526-1 | Danger Blues-1,-2 | Bluebird Unn. |
| 016527-1 | My Friend Has Forsaken Me-1,-2 | Bluebird B7416 |

016528-1	Mean Black Cat-1,-2	Bluebird B7303
016529-1	Brickyard-1,-2	Bluebird B7416
016530-1	Mamie Lee-1,-2	Bluebird B7386
016531-1	Take It Easy Baby-1	Bluebird B7386
016532-1	I Have Spent My Bonus-3	Bluebird B7303
016533-1	CNA-1,-3	Bluebird B7440

HENRY TOWNSEND
vcl/pno; Robert Lee McCoy, gtr; Sonny Boy Williamson, hra
Aurora, Ill. 11 November 1937

016534	Lose Your Man	Bluebird B7453
016535	All I've Got's Gone	Bluebird B7474
016536	A Ramblin' Mind	Bluebird B7474
016537	Now I Stay Away	Bluebird B4753

WALTER DAVIS
vcl/pno; Henry Townsend, gtr
Aurora, Ill. 19 December 1938

030828-1	I Like the Way You Spread Your Wings	Bluebird B7978
030829-1	Cuttin' Off My Days	Bluebird B7978
030830-1	You Don't Know Right from Wrong	Bluebird B8026
030831-1	Bad Luck and Trouble	Bluebird B8107
030832-1	Smokey Mountain	Bluebird B8026
030833-1	Your Time Is Comin'	Bluebird B8002
030834-1	Everything Is O.K.	Bluebird B8058
030835-1	Troubled and Weary	Bluebird B8107
030836-1	Early This Morning	Bluebird B8002
030837-1	Mercy Blues	Bluebird B8058

ST. LOUIS JIMMY
vcl-1; Henry Townsend, gtr/vcl-2; Roosevelt Sykes, pno; unk bs
Nashville, Tenn. 1949

UB2765B	I Ain't Done Nothing Wrong-1	Bullet 270
UB2768B	Going Down Slow-1	Bullet 270
	My Trouble-1	Bullet 278
	Sittin' and Thinkin'-1	Bullet 278
	Now I'm Through-2	Bullet 291
	Mr. Brown Boogie	Bullet 291

Note: It has been suggested that "Mr. Brown Boogie" featured pianist
Henry Brown on piano. Henry Townsend has identified the pianist as
Roosevelt Sykes.

ROOSEVELT SYKES
vcl/pno; poss Henry Townsend, gtr; unk tpt, ten, bs, dms
Nashville, Tenn. 1949

| 319A | Candy Man Blues | Bullet 319 |
| 319B | Why Should I Cry | Bullet 319 |

WALTER DAVIS
vcl/pno; Henry Townsend, gtr; unk ten-1, bs
Nashville, Tenn. 1949-50

	Move Back to the Woods	Bullet 305
	You've Got to Reap What You Sow	Bullet 305
	Wonder What I'm Doing Wrong	Bullet 311
	I Would Hate to Hate You	Bullet 311
	Santa Claus Blues	Bullet 321
	Got to See Her Every Night	Bullet 321
	So Long Baby-1	Bullet 326
	Stop That Train in Harlem-1	Bullet 326
	My Life Depends on You	Bullet 328
	Come on Baby	Bullet 328
	You Are the One I Love	Bullet 341
	I Just Can't Help It	Bullet 341
	Lonely Nights	Bullet 345
	Good Morning Baby	Bullet 345

WALTER DAVIS
vcl/pno; Henry Townsend, gtr; John Moore, ten
Chicago, Ill. 27 July 1952

E2VB-6864	You Make My World So Bright	Victor 20-5012
E2VB-6865	Tears Came Rollin' Down	Victor 20-5012
E2VB-6866	So Long Baby	Victor 20-5168
E2VB-6867	What May Your Trouble Be	Victor 20-5168

HENRY TOWNSEND
St. Louis, Mo. Summer 1960

| | spoken word | Decca LK 4664 |

Note: Interview material for *Conversation with the Blues,* produced by
Paul Oliver.

HENRY TOWNSEND
vcl/gtr/pno-1; Tommy Bankhead, gtr.
Technisonic Studios, St. Louis, Mo. 17 May 1961

Cairo's My Baby's Home	Bluesville BV1041
Tired of Being Mistreated	
Rocks Have Been My Pillow	
The Train Is Coming	
She Just Walked Away	
I Asked Her If She Loved Me	
I Got Tired	
My Home Ain't Here	
All My Money Gone-1	
She Drove Me to Drinking	
My Baby Have Come Back	

HENRY BROWN
speech/pno; Mike Stewart, gtr; Henry Townsend, speech
St. Louis, Mo. September 1969

Henry's Jive	Adelphi LP1012

HENRY TOWNSEND
vcl/gtr/pno-1; Andrew Cauthen, hra-2; Mike Stewart, gtr-1;
Clarence Johnson, vcl/gtr-3
St. Louis, Mo. September 1969

Cairo Blues	Adelphi LP1012
Tired of Being Mistreated-2	
Christmas Blues-1	
Baby Let Me Come Back Home-2,-3	

HENRY TOWNSEND
vcl/pno/gtr-1; Mike Stewart, gtr
St. Louis, Mo. September 1969

She Walked Away	Adelphi LP1016
Everyday of My Life-1	

HENRY TOWNSEND
vcl/gtr; Mike Stewart, gtr
Potomac, Md. August 1970

Biddle Street Blues	Adelphi LP1016
Sloppy Drunk Again	

HENRY TOWNSEND
vcl/gtr; Mike Stewart, gtr
Potomac, Md. August 1971

Buzz Buzz Buzz	Adelphi LP 1016
Doing Better in Life	
Don't You Remember Me	

HENRY TOWNSEND
vcl/gtr; Mike Stewart, gtr
Silver Spring, Md. August 1971

Now or Never	Adelphi LP 1016

HENRY TOWNSEND
vcl/gtr/pno-1; Henry Brown, pno-2; Vernell Townsend, vcl-3; Mike
Stewart, gtr-1
St. Louis, Mo. April 1974

Heart Trouble-1	Adelphi LP 1016
Deep Morgan Stomp-2	
Why Do We Love Each Other?-3	

HENRY TOWNSEND
vcl/gtr/pno-1
St. Louis, Mo. 23 January 1976

Tears Came Rolling Down	Red Lightnin' 0038
Wave My Hands Bye Bye-1	

Note: Recorded for the BBC series "The Devil's Music"

HENRY TOWNSEND
vcl/pno/gtr-1; Vernell Townsend, vcl-2; Yank Rachell, mdl-3/gtr-4;
Norman Merritt, gtr-5
St. Louis, Mo. 1979

Bad Luck Dice	Nighthawk 201
Nothing but Trouble	NHCD 202
Things Have Changed-3	
The Old Man's Soul	
Tears Come Rollin' Down-1,-2,-5	
It's a Hard Road to Travel	
Talkin' Guitar Blues-1,-4	
I'm Just an Ordinary Man	
Alley Strut	
Can't You See-1,-2	

Dark Clouds Rising-3
The Train Is at the Station
Overstayed My Time

HENRY TOWNSEND
vcl/gtr
Vienna, Austria. November 1980

Baby Please Don't Go	Wolf LP 120 495
Baby Tell Me, What Is on	Wolf CD 120-102
Your Mind	
Goodbye, Baby	
Cairo	
I Hate to Leave	
What Tomorrow Brings	
As She's Gone, I'm Looking Right	
in Her Heart	
Trying to Be Satisfied	

HENRY TOWNSEND AND VERNELL TOWNSEND
Henry Townsend, vcl/gtr/pno-1; Vernell Townsend, vcl-2
Kufstein, Austria. November 1980

Going Back Home-1	Wolf LP 120 495
M and O-1	Wolf CD 120-102
Going Down Slow-1,-2	
Early in the Morning	
Sloppy Drunk	
Tired of Being Mistreated	

HENRY TOWNSEND
vcl/gtr-1/pno-2
St. Louis, Mo. 11, 12, 15 August 1981

Hard Luck Story-1	Swingmaster 2107
The Cutback Blues-2	Swingmaster CD2201
Bring Me My Pistol and My	
Shotgun Too-1	
Heartbroken Man Blues-1	
Baby Boy Blues-1	
Tears Settled in My Eyes-1	
What Would You Do?-2	
The Three G's Blues-1	
Have No Fear-1	

           People Need People-2
           I Got to Go-1
           I'm Having Bad Luck-1

HENRY TOWNSEND
vcl/pno-1/gtr-2
St. Louis, Mo. 21 March 1983
           Too Pretty for Me-1   Swingmaster CD2201
           Your Doggone Ways-2

HENRY TOWNSEND
vcl/gtr
St. Louis, Mo. 23 March 1983
           Big City Blues   Swingmaster CD2201
           Dirty Trick Blues
           I'm Gonna Stay
           Hey Dear Brother
           Slap Her Down
           Down by That Muddy Pond

HENRY TOWNSEND AND VERNELL TOWNSEND
Henry Townsend, vcl/gtr-1/pno-2; Vernell Townsend, vcl-1
Atlanta, Ga. 19-21 October 1984
           The Tears Come Rolling Down-1   Southland SLP 24
           Standing Looking out the Window-2

HENRY TOWNSEND
vcl/pno
Groningen, Holland. 21 Nov. 1987
           Night Is Falling   Swingmaster CD2201

HENRY TOWNSEND
vcl/gtr; Ron Edwards, gtr
St. Louis, Mo., 1991
           Baby Please Don't Go   Blueberry Hill BBH-032
Note: Recorded on the radio program "Nothing but the Blues" on KDHX,
FM 88.1

HENRY TOWNSEND
vcl/gtr-1/pno-2; Ovell Manning, vcl-3; Scott Shuman, gtr-1; Mike
Melchione, bs-1; Dave Elliot, dms-4
Falls Church, Va., 1997

Drivin' the Highway (omit Townsend vcl)-1,-3	Blueberry Hill BBH-032
It's Got to End Somewhere-1	
Hear Me Cryin'-2	
Change Your Name-1,-4	

HENRY TOWNSEND
vcl/gtr-1/pno-2; Ron Edwards, gtr; John May, bs
St. Louis, Mo. 27-28 July 1997

I Believe in Love-1	Blueberry Hill BBH-032
No Doggin'-2	
Search Your Heart-1	
Train Comin'-1	
Gone Too Long-2	
Leave You Alone-2	
The Way You're Actin'-1	
The 88 Blues-2	
She's Gone-2 (omit Edwards and May)	

HENRY TOWNSEND
vcl/gtr; Leroy Pierson, gtr; John May, bs
St. Louis, Mo., 1997

You've Changed	Blueberry Hill BBH-032

Reissues featuring Henry Townsend's early recordings and those on
which he accompanies other artists:

Walter Davis, *Bluebird Vol. 9,* RCA INT 1085
Walter Davis, *The Bullet Sides,* Krazy Kat KK 7441
Walter Davis, *Think You Need a Shot,* RCA INT 1085
Cripple Clarence Lofton and Walter Davis, *Cripple Clarence Lofton/
Walter Davis,* Yazoo 1025
Roosevelt Sykes, *The Country Blues Piano Ace,* Yazoo 1033
Henry Townsend and Henry Spaulding, *Henry Townsend and Henry
Spaulding, 1929-37,* Wolf WSE117
Various Artists, *Best of Piano Blues,* Wolf CD 120-102
Various Artists, *Big Four,* Magpie PY 4412
Various Artists, *The Blues in St. Louis,* Origin OJL-20

Various Artists, *Central Highway,* Magpie PY 4413
Various Artists, *Good Time Blues,* Mamlish s3805
Various Artists, *Hard Time Blues,* Mamlish s3806
Various Artists, *St. Louis Blues, 1929–1935,* Yazoo 1030
Various Artists, *St. Louis Town, 1929–1932,* Yazoo 1003
Various Artists, *Times Are So Tight,* Swingtime 2017
Various Artists, *Too Late, Too Late,* Document CD 5411

BIBLIOGRAPHY

The following books, magazines, and liner notes were used to prepare for the interviews with Henry Townsend and also to compile the notes and discography.

Bastin, Bruce. *Never Sell a Copyright.* Chigwell, England: Storyville, 1990.

Dixon, Robert, and John Godrich. *Blues and Gospel Records, 1902–43.* Chigwell, England: Storyville, 1982.

Hall, Bob, and Richard Noblett. "A Handful of Keys." *Blues Unlimited* 112 (Mar.–Apr. 1975): 18.

Handy, W. C. *Father of the Blues.* New York: Da Capo Press, 1991.

Harris, Sheldon. *Blues Who's Who.* New Rochelle, N.Y.: Arlington House, 1979.

Leadbitter, Mike, and Slaven, Neil. *Blues Records, 1943–66.* London: Hanover, 1968.

Oliver, Paul. *Blues of the Record.* Tunbridge Wells, England: Baton Press, 1984.

———. *Conversation with the Blues.* London: Cassell, 1965.

———. *Story of the Blues.* London: Barrie and Rockliff, 1969.

Pierson, Leroy. Liner notes to *Mule* by Henry Townsend. Nighthawk LP 201. 1979.

Rowe, Mike. "Joe Dean from Bowling Green." *Blues Unlimited* 127 (Nov.–Dec. 1977): 4–9.

———. "Numerology Guide." *Blues Unlimited* 124 (May–June 1977): 11.

———. "St. Louis Had to Get Credit." *Blues Unlimited* 133 (Jan.–Feb. 1979): 4–10.

———. "Well Them Sparks Brothers They Been Here and Gone." *Blues Unlimited* 144 (May 1983): 9–14.

Rudwick, Elliot. *Race Riot at East St. Louis.* Carbondale: Southern Illinois University Press, 1964.

Stewart, Mike. "Backwards Sam in St. Louis." *Blues Unlimited* 72 (May 1970): 13–14.

Welding, Pete. "Henry Townsend." *Blues Unlimited* 57 (Nov. 1968): 11–12; 64 (July 1969): 11; 65 (Sept. 1969): 15; 66 (Oct. 1969): 9.

INDEX

Albany Hotel, 79, 94, 95, 124
Armstrong, Louis, 52, 116
Arnold, James Kokomo, 92, 124

Bailey, Red Mike, 53, 54, 118
Bankhead, Tommy, 108, 125
Barn, the (bar), 124
Barrelhouse Buck (Buck
 McFarland), 60, 120
Bates, Peg Leg, 17
B. B. (wholesale liquor salesman),
 67
Bekins Moving and Storage
 Company, 114
Bell, Red Eyed Jesse, 86
Berry, Chuck, 110
Betty and Molly's (speakeasy), 73
Blackwell, Scrapper, 71, 122
Blue (friend from 1920s), 8, 11, 17
Blue/Cookie (dancer), 101
Bluebird Records, 80, 82, 117, 123,
 124
Blue Heaven (speakeasy), 120
Blue Jay Central Cab, 93
Blunt, Annie, 1
Blunt, Lazarus, 1
Bogans, Pete, 25, 26, 28, 36, 63, 64,
 105, 115, 122
Booker Washington Hotel, 95
Booker Washington Theatre, 16,
 17, 18, 43, 113, 115
Boyd, Eddie ("Bowtie"), 91, 124
Boyd, Georgia, 56, 119
Bragg, Dobby (Roosevelt Sykes),
 55
Brent, Louis ("Slick"), 20, 114
Broonzy, Big Bill, 93

Brown, Henry, 58, 59, 62, 63, 64,
 87, 120
Brown, Hi Henry, 70, 121
Brown, Othum/Otha, 91, 124
Brown Mule (bar), 66
Brunswick Records, 36, 54, 120, 123
Bullet Records, 80, 123
Bumble Bee Slim (Amos Easton),
 92, 124
Butterbeans and Susie (vaudeville
 act), 17, 33

Callahan, Sergeant, 32
Calumet Hotel, 79, 95, 124
Carmichael, Roosevelt, 101, 102
Carr, Leroy, 38, 71, 73, 122
Carter, Oscar, 117
Chambers, Jordan, 11, 113
Charley Houston's (speakeasy), 34,
 43, 58, 63, 73
Charters, Sam, 108, 125
Checker Cab, 93
Chenier, Clifton, 5
Chesterfield Bar, 124
Clayton, Doctor, 92
Cleveland (neighborhood boss),
 96, 97
Cobb, Oliver, 51, 52, 53, 118
Columbia Records, 37, 38, 39,
 122
Cookie/Blue (dancer), 101
Corley, Cathy, 125
Corrine (girlfriend), 25, 29, 30
Countess, the (dancer), 101

Dance Box (night club), 34, 115
Darby, Blind Teddy, 72, 73

Davenport, Cow Cow, 38

Davis, Larry D., 114

Davis, Sergeant Thomas, 114

Davis, Walter, 39, 41, 43, 44, 54, 55,
    60, 61, 66, 74, 75, 76, 77, 78, 79,
    80, 86, 93, 94, 95, 96, 101, 102,
    105, 118, 122, 123

Davis, Will ("Otto"), 5, 6

Davis, Willie, 80

Dean, Joe, 57, 59, 63, 120

Decca Records, 119, 120, 121, 124

Delmark Records, 123

Deluxe Cabs, 116

Deluxe Cafe/Restaurant, 100, 116

Deluxe Hotel, 116

Deluxe Music Shoppe, 116

Deshay, James, 102

Dudlow, Joe ("Blue," "Harry"), 19,
    27, 28

Easton, Amos ("Bumble Bee
    Slim"), 92, 124

Eddie El (guitarist), 91, 124

Ellington, Duke, 116

Eskimo Inn, 32

Fanny (Minnow Townsend's and
    Sylvester Palmer's girlfriend),
    39

Fenster, Sam, 114

Fields, Willie ("Neckbones"), 49,
    61, 70, 120

Flamingo Inn, 93

Fletcher, Napoleon, 57, 119

Flowers, Dave, 11, 12

Foster, Ted, 113

Funky London (London The-
    ater), 8, 15, 17, 36, 40

Gabriel (St. Louis disk jockey),
    93, 103, 124

Gaslight Square, 123

Gibson, Clifford, 42, 55, 56, 103,
    117, 119

Glass Bar, 101, 124

Gordon, Jimmy, 59

Grand Central Hotel, 93, 94, 95,
    99, 124

Grand Theater, 33

Granite City Steel, 120

Green, Lee, 42, 43

Grimes, Fred, 99, 100

Hardin, Edith, 121

Hardin, Grady, 121

Hardin, Lane, 71, 121, 122

Hardin, William, 121

Harding, Joe, 60, 68

Hawkins, John M., 48, 49, 59

Hawkins, S. Q., 59

Henderson, Benjamin, 6

Hill, Emmett ("Humble Ser-
    vant"), 87

Hole in the Ground/Sadie's
    (speakeasy), 73

House, Son, 103

Humble Servant (Emmett Hill),
    87

Jazzland (night club), 41

J. C.'s (night club), 43

Jeeter-Pillars Band, 52

Jefferson, Blind Lemon, 19

Jim McMann's (speakeasy), 33

Joe's Corner (night club), 83

Joe's Music (store), 25, 114

Johnson, Clarence, 109, 125

Johnson, Eddie, 118

Johnson, Edith North, 53, 54, 57,
    116, 118, 119

Johnson, Harry, 53

Johnson, James ("Stump"), 54, 116

Johnson, Jesse, 17, 36, 37, 40, 42, 51, 54, 55, 57, 80, 100, 116

Johnson, Lonnie, 18, 19, 24, 35, 38, 54, 71, 90, 93, 111, 114, 125

Johnson, Mary, 36, 120

Johnson, Robert, 68, 69, 83, 121

Jones, Curtis, 91

Jordan, Charley, 37, 69, 121

Kelly, Willie (Roosevelt Sykes), 55

Keys, Dr. (African American physician), 8

Keys, Earl, 8, 11

King, Albert, 104, 124

King, B. B., 102, 110

Knapps (pianist), 57

Kohn, Sam, 114

Koonce, E. B., 9, 10, 113

Lay 'Em Straight (pianist), 63

Leadbelly (railroad detective), 23

Lewins Metal Company, 70

Little Walter, 91, 124

Lockwood, Robert, Jr., 92, 124

Lofton, Cripple Clarence, 92

London Theater (Funky London), 8, 15, 17, 36, 40

Lorraine (Archie Moore's mother), 29, 30

Lunceford, Jimmy, 116

Majestic Theater, 124

Martin (possible originator of "Cairo Blues"), 26

Maxim, Joey, 115

McAllister, Harvey, 88

McCoy, Ethel, 125

McCoy, George, 109, 125

McCoy, Joe, 125

McCoy, Robert Lee (Robert Nighthawk), 6, 79, 82, 83, 123

McFadden, Charlie ("Specks"), 44, 45, 46, 51, 117, 118

McFarland, Buck ("Barrelhouse Buck"), 60, 120

McKinnon/McKinley, Florence, 65

McKnight, Johnny, 33, 56, 62, 70

Melrose, Lester, 79, 122

Memphis Minnie, 61, 125

Memphis Slim, 87, 93, 123

Midtown Hotel, 124

Miller, Al, 68, 185

Miller, Aleck "Rice" ("Sonny Boy Williamson"), 103, 104, 105, 124

Miller, Eddie, 35, 36

Miller, Luella, 18, 35, 36, 54, 115

Minnesota Fats, 87

Miss Callie's (speakeasy), 46, 101

Montgomery, Little Brother, 42

Moore, Alice, 58, 63, 119, 120

Moore, Archie, 29, 30, 115

Moore, Johnny, 101, 102

Morris, James, 65

Murphy, Matt ("Guitar"), 87, 93, 123

Mushlin, Maurice, 124

Neckbones (Willie Fields), 49, 61, 70, 120

Nettie's (speakeasy), 63

Nighthawk, Robert (Robert Lee McCoy), 6, 79, 82, 83, 123

Nina (prostitute), 98

Oberstein, Eli, 122

Oden, James Burke ("St. Louis Jimmy"), 71, 72, 86, 92, 122, 123

Okeh Records, 36, 37, 42, 115, 117, 119

Ora-Nelle Records, 124

Palmer, Amanda, 116
Palmer, Sylvester, 37, 38, 39, 116
Paradise Dance Palace, 118
Paramount Records, 36, 51, 53, 80, 117, 118, 119, 120, 124
Patterson, Teenie Mae, 93
Pearchfield, Dave, 19, 25
Peeples, Robert, 116
Pegg, Johnny, 31, 32
Peoples Undertaking Co., 113
Perryman, Rufus ("Speckled Red"), 86, 123
Pinkie (guitarist), 91
Promnitz, Walter (patrolman), 114

QRS Records, 117

Rafferty, Carl, 57, 119
Rainey, Ma, 17, 113
Randle, Eddie, 52, 118
Randolph, Edward, 120
Riviera (night club), 113
Rogers, Ike, 58, 63, 64, 120
Royal Candy Kitchen (speakeasy), 43
Ryan, Son, 19, 25, 26

Sadie's/Hole in the Ground (speakeasy), 73
Salt and Pepper Shakers (band), 118
Sam (trumpeter), 63
Scarfino (whiskey seller), 67
Scruggs, Baby, 115
Scruggs, Irene, 36, 115
Searcy, Deloise, 34, 35
Short, J. D. ("Jelly Jaw"), 46, 47, 48, 49, 50, 56, 82, 117
Show Bar, 124
Smith, Bessie, 17, 113

Smith, Bessie Mae ("St. Louis Bessie"), 58, 116, 119
Smith, Clara, 113, 115
Sortier, Ann, 83
Sparks, Aaron ("Pinetop"), 63, 64, 73, 87, 119
Sparks, Jimmie Lee, 63
Sparks, Marion (Milton, Lindberg), 63, 64, 120
Spaulding, Henry, 19, 26, 42, 54, 61, 62, 114
Speckled Red (Rufus Perryman), 86, 123
Spivey, Victoria, 36, 116
Starr Piano Company, 80
St. Louis Bessie (Bessie Mae Smith), 58, 116, 119
St. Louis Crackerjacks (band), 115, 118
St. Louis Jimmy (James Burke Oden), 71, 72, 86, 92, 122, 123
Storyville Records, 123
Sunnyland Slim, 92
Sykes, Isabel, 57, 119
Sykes, Jesse, 41, 46, 86
Sykes, Johnny, 41
Sykes, Leola, 44
Sykes, Marion, 57
Sykes, Roosevelt, 33–36, 40–46, 51, 53–58, 61–64, 71, 72, 74, 83–87, 90, 92, 93, 102–5, 111, 116, 117, 118, 119, 122, 123
Sykes, Rufus, 85
Sykes, Walter, 41, 86, 117
Sykes, Willie, 41

Tampa Red, 83, 93, 115
Taylor, William, 120
Telphy, James, 118
T. J.'s (gambling hall), 48
Tobacco George's (night club), 84

Townsend, Allen (father), 1, 114

Townsend, Amelia Blunt (mother), 1, 114

Townsend, Charley (brother), 3, 5

Townsend, James (uncle), 1

Townsend, Jesse (uncle), 1

Townsend, Lazarus ("Minnow," brother), 3, 4, 12, 39, 55, 107, 118

Townsend, Luke (uncle), 1

Townsend, Marie (sister-in-law), 107

Townsend, Nina (wife), 105, 106

Townsend, Vernell (wife), 57, 80, 106, 107, 110, 124

Trowbridge, Dorothea, 57, 58, 119

Turner, Lizzie, 121

Turpin, Charles, 17, 113, 114

Victor Records/RCA Victor, 36, 42, 54, 80, 117, 118, 122, 123

Vocalion Records, 117, 119, 121, 124

Walker, Ernest, 68, 121

Walker, T-Bone, 110

Wallace, Wesley, 39, 40, 116

Warschosky Rubber Plant, 22

Washboard Sam, 82, 123

Waters, Muddy, 83, 93, 112, 124

Watts, Eva, 8, 11

Webb, Tommy, 72

West End Hotel, 79, 99, 124

West End Waiters (theater), 101, 124

Wheatstraw, Peetie, 40, 56, 60, 61, 62, 70, 120

White, Willie, 75, 122

Wilkins, Joe Willie, 83, 84, 103, 124

Williams, Big Joe, 73, 74, 79, 81, 82, 84, 86, 122, 123

Williams, Clarence, 38

Williams, Dave, 3, 4

Williams, Ike, 4

Williams, Irene, 3, 4

Williams, Jabo, 33, 62, 120

Williams, Samuel ("Sambo"), 62

Williams, Tobe, 49, 61

Williamson, John Lee ("Sonny Boy"), 18, 81, 82, 83, 86, 91, 92, 93, 103, 123, 124

Williamson, Lacy Belle, 81, 93

Williamson, Sonny Boy (Aleck "Rice" Miller), 103, 104, 105, 124

Williamson, Sonny Boy (John Lee Williamson), 18, 81, 82, 83, 86, 91, 92, 93, 103, 123, 124

Winchester, Pete, 23

Wisconsin Chair Company, 117

Wolff, Sam, 25, 37, 114

Wolff's Music Shop, 25, 37, 114

Wrights, Robert, 34, 35

MUSIC IN AMERICAN LIFE

Only a Miner: Studies in Recorded Coal-Mining Songs   *Archie Green*

Great Day Coming: Folk Music and the American Left   *R. Serge Denisoff*

John Philip Sousa: A Descriptive Catalog of His Works   *Paul E. Bierley*

The Hell-Bound Train: A Cowboy Songbook   *Glenn Ohrlin*

Oh, Didn't He Ramble: The Life Story of Lee Collins, as Told to
   Mary Collins   *Edited by Frank J. Gillis and John W. Miner*

American Labor Songs of the Nineteenth Century   *Philip S. Foner*

Stars of Country Music: Uncle Dave Macon to Johnny Rodriguez
   Edited by Bill C. Malone and Judith McCulloh

Git Along, Little Dogies: Songs and Songmakers of the American West
   John I. White

A Texas-Mexican *Cancionero:* Folksongs of the Lower Border   *Américo Paredes*

San Antonio Rose: The Life and Music of Bob Wills   *Charles R. Townsend*

Early Downhome Blues: A Musical and Cultural Analysis   *Jeff Todd Titon*

An Ives Celebration: Papers and Panels of the Charles Ives Centennial
   Festival-Conference   *Edited by H. Wiley Hitchcock and Vivian Perlis*

Sinful Tunes and Spirituals: Black Folk Music to the Civil War   *Dena J. Epstein*

Joe Scott, the Woodsman-Songmaker   *Edward D. Ives*

Jimmie Rodgers: The Life and Times of America's Blue Yodeler
   Nolan Porterfield

Early American Music Engraving and Printing: A History of Music
   Publishing in America from 1787 to 1825, with Commentary on Earlier
   and Later Practices   *Richard J. Wolfe*

Sing a Sad Song: The Life of Hank Williams   *Roger M. Williams*

Long Steel Rail: The Railroad in American Folksong   *Norm Cohen*

Resources of American Music History: A Directory of Source Materials from
   Colonial Times to World War II   *D. W. Krummel, Jean Geil, Doris J. Dyen,
   and Deane L. Root*

Tenement Songs: The Popular Music of the Jewish Immigrants   *Mark Slobin*

Ozark Folksongs   *Vance Randolph; edited and abridged by Norm Cohen*

Oscar Sonneck and American Music   *Edited by William Lichtenwanger*

Bluegrass Breakdown: The Making of the Old Southern Sound
   Robert Cantwell

Bluegrass: A History   *Neil V. Rosenberg*

Music at the White House: A History of the American Spirit   *Elise K. Kirk*

Red River Blues: The Blues Tradition in the Southeast   *Bruce Bastin*

Good Friends and Bad Enemies: Robert Winslow Gordon and the Study of
   American Folksong   *Debora Kodish*

Fiddlin' Georgia Crazy: Fiddlin' John Carson, His Real World, and the World
    of His Songs   *Gene Wiggins*
America's Music: From the Pilgrims to the Present (rev. 3d ed.)   *Gilbert Chase*
Secular Music in Colonial Annapolis: The Tuesday Club, 1745–56
    John Barry Talley
Bibliographical Handbook of American Music   *D. W. Krummel*
Goin' to Kansas City   *Nathan W. Pearson, Jr.*
"Susanna," "Jeanie," and "The Old Folks at Home": The Songs of
    Stephen C. Foster from His Time to Ours (2d ed.)   *William W. Austin*
Songprints: The Musical Experience of Five Shoshone Women   *Judith Vander*
"Happy in the Service of the Lord": Afro-American Gospel Quartets in
    Memphis   *Kip Lornell*
Paul Hindemith in the United States   *Luther Noss*
"My Song Is My Weapon": People's Songs, American Communism, and the
    Politics of Culture, 1930–50   *Robbie Lieberman*
Chosen Voices: The Story of the American Cantorate   *Mark Slobin*
Theodore Thomas: America's Conductor and Builder of Orchestras,
    1835–1905   *Ezra Schabas*
"The Whorehouse Bells Were Ringing" and Other Songs Cowboys Sing
    Guy Logsdon
Crazeology: The Autobiography of a Chicago Jazzman   *Bud Freeman,
    as Told to Robert Wolf*
Discoursing Sweet Music: Brass Bands and Community Life in
    Turn-of-the-Century Pennsylvania   *Kenneth Kreitner*
Mormonism and Music: A History   *Michael Hicks*
Voices of the Jazz Age: Profiles of Eight Vintage Jazzmen   *Chip Deffaa*
Pickin' on Peachtree: A History of Country Music in Atlanta, Georgia
    Wayne W. Daniel
Bitter Music: Collected Journals, Essays, Introductions, and Librettos
    Harry Partch; edited by Thomas McGeary
Ethnic Music on Records: A Discography of Ethnic Recordings Produced in
    the United States, 1893 to 1942   *Richard K. Spottswood*
Downhome Blues Lyrics: An Anthology from the Post-World War II Era
    Jeff Todd Titon
Ellington: The Early Years   *Mark Tucker*
Chicago Soul   *Robert Pruter*
That Half-Barbaric Twang: The Banjo in American Popular Culture
    Karen Linn
Hot Man: The Life of Art Hodes   *Art Hodes and Chadwick Hansen*
The Erotic Muse: American Bawdy Songs (2d ed.)   *Ed Cray*

Barrio Rhythm: Mexican American Music in Los Angeles   *Steven Loza*

The Creation of Jazz: Music, Race, and Culture in Urban America
   Burton W. Peretti

Charles Martin Loeffler: A Life Apart in Music   *Ellen Knight*

Club Date Musicians: Playing the New York Party Circuit   *Bruce A. MacLeod*

Opera on the Road: Traveling Opera Troupes in the United States,
   1825–60   *Katherine K. Preston*

The Stonemans: An Appalachian Family and the Music That Shaped
   Their Lives   *Ivan M. Tribe*

Transforming Tradition: Folk Music Revivals Examined
   Edited by Neil V. Rosenberg

The Crooked Stovepipe: Athapaskan Fiddle Music and Square Dancing
   in Northeast Alaska and Northwest Canada   *Craig Mishler*

Traveling the High Way Home: Ralph Stanley and the World of Traditional
   Bluegrass Music   *John Wright*

Carl Ruggles: Composer, Painter, and Storyteller   *Marilyn Ziffrin*

Never without a Song: The Years and Songs of Jennie Devlin,
   1865–1952   *Katharine D. Newman*

The Hank Snow Story   *Hank Snow, with Jack Ownbey and Bob Burris*

Milton Brown and the Founding of Western Swing   *Cary Ginell, with
   special assistance from Roy Lee Brown*

Santiago de Murcia's "Códice Saldívar No. 4": A Treasury of Secular Guitar
   Music from Baroque Mexico   *Craig H. Russell*

The Sound of the Dove: Singing in Appalachian Primitive Baptist
   Churches   *Beverly Bush Patterson*

Heartland Excursions: Ethnomusicological Reflections on Schools
   of Music   *Bruno Nettl*

Doowop: The Chicago Scene   *Robert Pruter*

Blue Rhythms: Six Lives in Rhythm and Blues   *Chip Deffaa*

Shoshone Ghost Dance Religion: Poetry Songs and Great Basin
   Context   *Judith Vander*

Go Cat Go! Rockabilly Music and Its Makers   *Craig Morrison*

'Twas Only an Irishman's Dream: The Image of Ireland and the Irish in
   American Popular Song Lyrics, 1800–1920   *William H. A. Williams*

Democracy at the Opera: Music, Theater, and Culture in New York City,
   1815–60   *Karen Ahlquist*

Fred Waring and the Pennsylvanians   *Virginia Waring*

Woody, Cisco, and Me: Seamen Three in the Merchant Marine   *Jim Longhi*

Behind the Burnt Cork Mask: Early Blackface Minstrelsy and Antebellum
   American Popular Culture   *William J. Mahar*

Going to Cincinnati: A History of the Blues in the Queen City   *Steven C. Tracy*
Pistol Packin' Mama: Aunt Molly Jackson and the Politics of Folksong
    Shelly Romalis
Sixties Rock: Garage, Psychedelic, and Other Satisfactions   *Michael Hicks*
The Late Great Johnny Ace and the Transition from R&B to
    Rock 'n' Roll   *James M. Salem*
Tito Puente and the Making of Latin Music   *Steven Loza*
Juilliard: A History   *Andrea Olmstead*
Understanding Charles Seeger, Pioneer in American Musicology
    Edited by Bell Yung and Helen Rees
Mountains of Music: West Virginia Traditional Music from *Goldenseal*
    Edited by John Lilly
Alice Tully: An Intimate Portrait   *Albert Fuller*
A Blues Life   *Henry Townsend, as Told to Bill Greensmith*

Typeset in 10.8/15 Adobe Caslon

with Smokler display

Designed by Richard Hendel

Composed by Jim Proefrock

at the University of Illinois Press

Manufactured by Thomson-Shore, Inc.

University of Illinois Press

1325 South Oak Street

Champaign, Illinois 61820-6903

www.press.uillinois.edu